History Source Books

The Middle Ages Book **4**

England and France

Peter & Mary Speed

Oxford University Press 1989

Oxford University Press, Walton Street, Oxford OX2 6DP
Oxford New York Toronto
Delhi Bombay Calcutta Madras Karachi
Petaling Jaya Singapore Hong Kong Tokyo
Nairobi Dar es Salaam Cape Town
Melbourne Auckland

and associated companies in
Berlin Ibadan

ISBN 0 19 917133 5

Typeset by Best Set Typesetters, Hong Kong
Printed in Hong Kong

Acknowledgements

The publishers would like to thank the following for permission to reproduce the photographs:

The picture on p 45 right is reproduced by Gracious Permission of Her Majesty the Queen;
Bibliothèque Nationale, Paris, cover, pp 17, 23, 32, 37, 57, 65 (Bibliothèque Arsenal), 70, 75 (Bibliothèque Arsenal), 78; Bodleian Library, Oxford, pp 21 (Ms Laud Misc 653 f7), 68–9 (Ms Bodley 264 f222r); British Library, pp 2–3, 6 right, 7, 9 bottom, 10, 25 top, 31, 39, 45 left, 46 bottom, 48, 51, 56, 60 (Weidenfeld and Nicolson Archives), 62, 63 top, 80; The Syndics of Cambridge University Library, pp 9 top (Ms Ee.3.59), 24–5 ('Essenwein Mittelalterliches Hausbuch' 1887); Governing Body of Christ Church Oxford, p 47; Fitzwilliam Museum, Cambridge, p 30; Giraudon, pp 52, 66 left, 67 and 71 (both Bibliothèque Nationale), 76 (Archives Municipales Toulouse) 77 (Bibliothèque Municipale Rouen), 79 right; Mansell Collection, pp 5 left, 63 bottom, 66 right, 79 left; Andrew Miller, p 38; Musée des Beaux-Arts de Dijon, p 72; Musées Nationaux Paris, p 73; National Maritime Museum London, p 28; M W Norris, pp 4 right, 5 right, 58; Graham Payne, p 61 (from Robert Hardy 'Longbow'); The Board of Trustees of the Royal Armouries, p 5 bottom; Royal Commission on the Historical Monuments of England, pp 12, 46 top; Trustees of the Science Museum London, p 29; Peter Speed, pp 11, 26, 34, 49; Stephen Turnbull, p 74; Trustees of the Wallace Collection, p 6 left; The Dean and Chapter of Westminster, p 59.

Picture Research by Sandra Assersohn

Illustrations by Martin Cox, Richard Hook and Christine Molan.

Contents

1 War in the Middle Ages

A Arms and Armour

The Knight and his Armour

During the early Middle Ages, knights wore mail armour. Mail was made of hundreds of tiny rings, joined together. It looked a bit like knitting that had been done with wire, instead of wool (Figure 1).

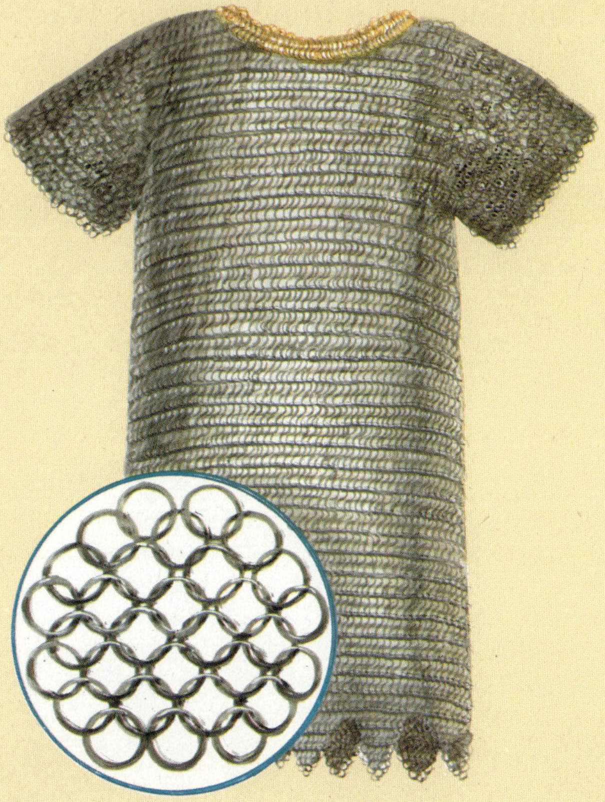

Figure 1 Mail

Mail gave quite good protection, but if it was struck, the blow did not glance off. Instead, the point of the weapon would stick in the mesh. Indeed, if the blow was hard enough, the sword, spear, or arrow might go through the mail, and drive pieces of it into the wound.

In the fourteenth century, archers became very dangerous and knights had to improve their armour. At first, they did so by fitting pieces of metal over their mail. Look at the knight in Figure 2. Find the pieces of metal which he has over his mail. Which parts of his body do they protect?

After a time, craftsmen discovered how to make armour from sheets of steel. This is

Figure 2 Brass of Sir William Fitzralph, 1323, Pebmarsh Church, Essex. The long, flowing garment made from cloth is a 'surcoat'. It was only for show. Its skirts could be a nuisance, especially in a fight.

called 'plate armour'. By the end of the fourteenth century, suits of armour were almost entirely of plate. They had very little mail in them. Look at Figures 3 and 4. The Black Prince has some mail round his neck, but nowhere else. Sir Thomas Swynborne, who lived a little later, has no mail at all. His body is completely covered with steel.

It is quite easy to decide when a suit of armour was made:

1 About 1300 or earlier – all of mail, apart from the helmet.
2 About 1400 or later – all of plate.
3 Between 1300 and 1400 – some mail, and some plate. The more plate there is, the later it is in this century.

A knight wearing plate armour was much safer than one wearing mail. But he still might be hurt. For example, if an arrow hit a joint in the armour it might well go through it. What do we mean, today, when we say someone 'has a chink in his armour'?

An important part of the armour was the helmet. Look at Figure 5. This helmet has a visor, which the knight can raise when he wants to see more clearly. Find the pivot on which the visor turns. The visor comes to a point, so that any blows to it will glance off. Why does the visor have a slit in it, do you think? Why does it have a lot of small holes?

A suit of armour was heavy. It could weigh as much as thirty kilograms. But the joints were so well made that it was quite easy to move. It is said that King Henry V could vault on to his horse, when he was wearing his armour. A few years ago some people in New York experimented with suits of armour. They put them on and found they could run, jump, lie down and stand up, all quite easily.

Early in the fourteenth century knights carried shields. But the Black Prince does not have one, nor does Sir Thomas Swynborne. Neither of them would have felt he needed a shield. Why was that, do you suppose? (Think of the changes there had been in armour.)

Figure 3 (left) Effigy of the Black Prince, 1376, Canterbury Cathedral. Like Sir William Fitzralph (Fig. 2), the Black Prince has a cloth garment over his armour. But this is a 'jupon'. How is it different from a surcoat?

Figure 4 Brass of Sir Thomas Swynborne, 1420, Little Horkesley, Essex. This knight has no cloth garment over his armour. To make a show, he would have had his armour polished until it shone.

Knights had several different kinds of weapons. However, the most common were the ones you can see in the pictures. What are they?

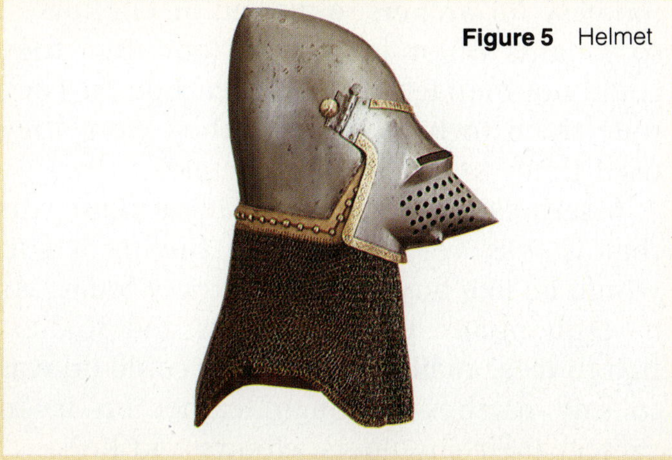

Figure 5 Helmet

Figure 6 (left)
Knight on horseback

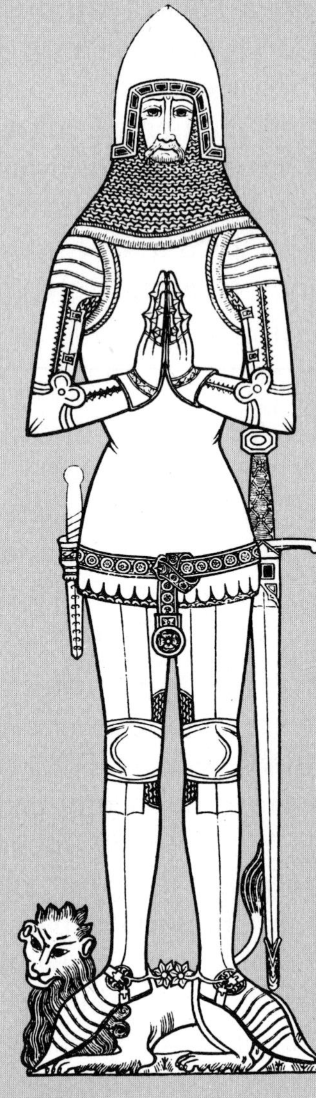

Figure 7 Brass of
Sir John Bettesthorne,
Mere, Wiltshire

Figure 6 shows a knight on his horse. The horse has some armour, but not nearly enough to cover him completely. It was only too easy for archers to wound or kill horses, so knights often fought on foot. But they could not manage without their horses. They rode them to battle, and, if they won, they used them to chase their enemies.

A serious problem with plate armour was that is was very expensive. Buying a suit would be like buying a Rolls Royce today. As a result, many poorer knights and soldiers had to wear mail. The best they could do was to sew patches of tough leather on it, to protect their shoulders, elbows and knees.

1 What armour replaced mail in the fourteenth century?
2 Why did knights often fight on foot?
3 Look at Figure 7. Was this knight's armour made in about 1320, 1390 or 1420? Given reasons for your answer.

Archers

There were many archers in the army which William the Conqueror brought to England in 1066. They did a great deal to help him win the Battle of Hastings. These men used the short bow, which was about a metre and a half long, and was drawn to the chest. It was a dangerous weapon, but not as deadly as the long bow. This was nearly two metres long, and was drawn right back to the ear. The English first met the long bow when they tried to conquer South Wales. Here are some stories about the Welsh archers, told by a Welsh clergyman:

Document One

The people of South Wales are excellent archers, as these examples prove. In an attack on a castle, two soldiers were running to take refuge in a tower when the Welsh shot at them. Their arrows penetrated the oak door of the tower, which was four inches thick. The arrows are still in the door today, in memory of the event. An English nobleman says that, when fighting the Welsh, one of his soldiers was wounded by an arrow. It went through his thigh, and the armour on both sides of it, and then so far through the saddle that it mortally wounded the horse. Another soldier had his hip, also protected by armour, pierced by an arrow which went into his saddle. On turning his horse, he had a similar wound in the opposite hip, which fixed him to both sides of his seat.

Giraldus Cambrensis, *Itinerary Through Wales*

Do you believe these stories? But whether they are true or not, it is certain that the English were very impressed by the long bow. The proof is, that they decided to use it themselves. Their problem was that the long bow is a difficult weapon. It takes years to learn how to shoot it well. Even then the archer must keep on practising. As a result, Parliament often made laws like this:

Document Two

No person shall use any unlawful plays, such as dice, football, and such like plays. But every man mighty and able in body should use his bow, because the defence of this land standeth much by Archers.

Rotuli Parliamentorum

1 What games must people not play?
2 What must they do instead?
3 What is the reason for this law?

Figure 8 Archers

Figure 8 shows some archers in battle. You can see that their bows are taller than they are, and that they are drawing them back to the ear. The archer wears a mail shirt with a leather jerkin over it.

1 The mail shirt only has short sleeves. Why is that, do you think?
2 How is the archer's helmet different from the knight's?
3 What weapon does the archer carry as well as his bow?

A good long bowman could hit his target at a distance of 250 metres. Also, he could shoot twelve arrows a minute. Even a small body of archers could deliver a shower of arrows that seemed to fall as fast as rain drops. It is not surprising that knights wanted plate armour, and that many of them would not take their horses into battle.

Archers were quite humble men. Many were yeomen, who owned small farms. But in battle they mattered more than the knights. Thanks to its archers, the English army was the best in Europe.

B Fighting a Battle

In 1402 the Scots and the English fought the Battle of Halidon Hill. An English monk describes it:

Document One

The Scots chose a hill where they gathered their knights and archers. At once, our archers, who were in the valley, shot arrows at the Scots to provoke them to come down. In reply, the Scottish archers fired as hard as they could at our archers. But our arrows fell on them like a shower of rain, and they fled.

The Earl of Douglas, who was the leader of the Scots, did not want his whole army to run away. He seized a lance, and rode down the hill with a troop of horse. He hoped to rush on our archers. He trusted too much in his equipment and that of his men, who had been improving their armour for three years.

When our archers saw the Scots charging, they retreated. But they went on firing so fast and so well that they pierced the armour and helmets and split the lances of the Scots, all with great ease. The Earl of Douglas was wounded five times, in spite of his fine armour. The rest of the Scots, who had not come down the hill, turned tail and fled. But this did them no good, since the archers followed them and they were forced to give themselves up, for fear of the death-dealing arrows. The Earl of Douglas was captured, many of those that fled were captured, but many were drowned in the River Tweed.

God gave this victory to the English archers alone. Our nobles and knights were no more than idle spectators of the battle.

Thomas Walsingham, *Historia Anglicana*

1 Where did the Scots gather their army?
2 The English and the Scottish archers fought each other. Which side won?
3 What did the Earl of Douglas hope to do?
4 How had the Scots been improving their armour, do you suppose? (Remember what you read in the last section.)
5 In what ways did the English archers hurt the Scottish knights?
6 How many times was the Earl of Douglas wounded? What happened to him, in the end?
7 What happened to many of the Scots?
8 What part did the English nobles and knights play in the battle?

Not all battles were like Halidon Hill. Quite often knights fought against one another. This extract describes such a fight:

Document Two

It is a marvellous and terrifying thing to hear the thundering of horses' hooves, the cries of the wounded, the shouting of war cries. The tumult and noise are heard at a distance of ten miles. And it is a great grief to see the finest of all the nobles and knights go to destruction and to death on both sides.

Froissart, *The Chronicles*

1 What are the noises of battle?
2 How far do these noises carry?
3 What is it sad to see?

This is how a man may feel during a battle:

Document Three

You will often be afraid when you see your enemies bearing down on you, with lances lowered to strike you, and swords ready to attack you. Arrows fly at you, and you do not know how to protect yourself. Now you see men slaughtering one another, flying, dying and being taken prisoner. You see your friends dead, whose corpses lie before you.

Your horses, though, are not killed. You could easily escape. But if you flee, you dishonour yourself; if you stay, you will have honour ever after.

Le Livre de Monsieur Geoffroi de Charny

1 What are some of the things that will frighten a man during a battle?
2 What, if anything, will stop him from running away?

Figure 1 and **2** Battles between knights. What weapons are the knights using? One of these pictures was drawn in about 1250, and the other in about 1450. Say which is which, and give reasons for your answer. (Read the first few paragraphs of 'The Knight and his Armour' in the last section.)

C Ransom

In 1338 the French burnt Southampton. During the fighting a French knight was captured by an English peasant. Hoping to save his life, the knight cried 'Rançon, rançon!' Probably you can guess what he meant, but the peasant did not understand him. 'Yes,' he said, 'I know you're a Frenchman,' and he cut his throat. None of the soldiers fighting in France would have made the same mistake as this peasant. They all knew that rich prisoners could be made to pay high ransoms.

The most valuable prisoner ever taken was probably King John II of France. He was captured at the Battle of Poitiers in 1356, by Sir Denis de Morbeke.

When the English commander, the Black Prince, heard that the King was captured, he sent the Earl of Warwick and Sir Raymond Cobham to look for him. This is what happened:

Document One

The two lords rode up a little hill to look about them. Then they saw a crowd of soldiers coming towards them. Among them was the French King, on foot and in great danger, for Englishmen and Gascons were his masters. They had taken him from Sir Denis de Morbeke by force and were all shouting, 'I have taken him! I have taken him!' The French King, to save himself, said, 'Sirs, lead me to the Prince, and do not argue about who took me. I am so great a lord, I can make you all rich.' However,

Figure 1 The Duke of Orleans in the Tower of London. The Duke was captured at Agincourt in 1415. His ransom was so huge that he could not pay it and he was held prisoner for 25 years. However, he did not suffer too much. He went hawking and hunting, he ate the best of food and he slept in a comfortable bed, with silk sheets. Much of his time he spent writing poetry, which is what he is doing here.

they still went on rioting and bellowing that they had taken the King. Then the Earl of Warwick and Sir Richard Cobham went into the crowd and made every man draw back. They ordered them, in the Prince's name, and on pain of losing their heads, to make no more noise, and to keep away from the King.
Froissart, *The Chronicles*

1 Who had taken the King from Sir Denis de Morbeke? What were they shouting?
2 Why was the King in danger?
3 How was he saved?

So many men claimed to have captured King John that Edward III of England thought the fairest thing would be to keep the ransom for himself! This was fixed at £500,000, in their money. It is impossible to say what that would be worth now, but it would be at least a hundred times as much. What do we mean today, when we say something is 'worth a king's ransom'?

After the Battle of Poitiers, where King John was captured, many of the French ran away. This is what happened to one of them:

Document Two

It happened that a squire of Picardy called John de Hellenes fled from the battle. He was chased by Lord Berkeley of England, a brave young knight. When they had gone about a league, John turned, and came riding towards Lord Berkeley, who raised his sword to strike the squire. But John dodged the stroke, and the Englishman missed him. Then, as he passed, John struck Lord Berkeley on the arm, and his sword fell on to the ground. He dismounted from his horse, and stooped down to take up his sword. At this, the French squire thrust at him with his own sword. He pierced the knight through both his thighs, so that he fell on the earth and could not move. And John got off his horse, and took the knight's sword, and asked him if he would yield. 'Well', said the knight, 'I am willing to be your prisoner, for you have won me in a fair fight.' Then he swore to be his prisoner, rescue or no rescue.

The squire drew the sword out of the knight's thighs. Then he bound the wound and got him a litter and so brought him in comfort to his house in Picardy. There he stayed for more than a year, until his wounds healed. And when he left, he paid for his ransom 6000 nobles. And the squire was made a knight because of the money he had from Lord Berkeley.
Froissart, *The Chronicles.*

Figure 2 Farleigh Castle, Somerset. Walter, Lord Hungerford, captured eight valuable prisoners at Agincourt. The money from their ransoms paid for the building of this castle.

Notes: 'squire' – man who is preparing to become a knight
'noble'– coin worth a third of £1. Perhaps worth between £30 and £50 today

1 Describe, in your own words, the fight between John de Hellenes and Lord Berkeley.
2 Why did John de Hellenes help Lord Berkeley so carefully, do you suppose?
3 How much was Lord Berkeley's ransom?
4 What did John de Hellenes become, as a result of making all this money?

2 The Hundred Years War to 1415

Figure 1 Edward III

A Introduction

During the early Middle ages the kings of England were also rulers of much of France. Henry II (1154–1189) owned more of France than the French king. Then, bit by bit, the kings of England lost most of their French possessions. By the early fourteenth century, all that remained were the lands shown on the map. But Gascony in the south-west of France was important for England. The Gascons were good customers for English wool, which they exchanged for wine. Also, they paid a lot of taxes. The kings of England were determined to keep Gascony. They also wanted to take as much more of France as they could. These ambitions led to the Hundred Years War. It began in 1337, during the reign of Edward III. We will ask one of his nobles to tell us about it.

'How did the war begin?'

'Our King, Edward III, claimed that he was the rightful King of France. The French would not have him, so he attacked them.'

'What happened in the war?'

'It started by French ships raiding the coast of England. They burnt Southampton to the ground. But we had our revenge in 1340. Our fleet defeated a great French fleet at Sluys.'

'Was there any fighting on land?'

'Our King found some allies in Flanders, and together we invaded the north of France. However, our allies did not help us as they should have done. The invasion was a failure. But 1346 was a great year for us.'

'What happened?'

'King Edward invaded Normandy. The French tried to stop him at Crécy, but he defeated them soundly. It was a splendid victory, since the French outnumbered us several times. The King's eldest son, the Black Prince, won fame that day. He had charge of one the divisions of our army. He led it with great skill and did many brave deeds. He was only sixteen at the time, but an experienced soldier could not have done better.

After winning the Battle of Crécy, the King took his army to besiege Calais. The town fell the next year. That meant we now had an important port, quite close to England.'

'Were there any more big battles?'

'Yes, indeed. In 1356 the Black Prince led an army into the heart of France. A huge French army caught him near Poitiers and forced him to give battle. The English were heavily outnumbered, but they won. Not only that, the King of France, John II, was taken prisoner. The Black Prince brought him in triumph to London.

In 1360 the French decided to make peace. They signed a treaty with us at Brétigny.'

'Did that mean Edward III became King of France?'

'No. He gave up his title to the throne. But the French agreed that he could keep Calais, and a great deal of land in the south-west of France. He did not have the whole kingdom, but he was master of a third of it.'

Peace did not last for long. War broke out again in 1369. France now had an able king, Charles V. He appointed an excellent general,

Bertrand du Guesclin. Du Guesclin saw it was a mistake for the French to try and defeat the English in battle. Instead, he wore the English down by guerrilla warfare. His men shadowed the English armies. They killed stragglers and attacked scouting parties and other small, isolated bands. Also, wherever the English were, the French cleared the countryside of food. Hunger and disease then killed far more of the English than would ever have died in battle. Their armies just wasted away.

There was one important battle, but it took place at sea. At that time, France had an alliance with one of the Spanish kingdoms, Castille. In 1372 the Earl of Pembroke was taking an army by sea to defend Gascony. A Castilian fleet caught him off La Rochelle and defeated him. Pembroke's army was lost, along with his fleet and Gascony was at the mercy of the French. They soon overran most of it.

By 1375 Edward III still had Calais. But in south-west France he held no more land than at the start of the war. In 1376 the Black Prince died, worn out by the fighting. Edward himself died the following year.

1 What province in south-west France belonged to the king of England in the early fourteenth century?
2 How did the Hundred Years War begin?
3 What naval battle did the English win in 1340?
4 What town did the English capture in 1347?
5 How much of France did Edward III gain by the Treaty of Brétigny?
6 Who was Charles V's general?
7 What kind of warfare did he wage?
8 Who defeated the English at sea in 1372?
9 What did this victory allow the French to do?

Figure 2 English possessions in France in the early fourteenth century

Figure 3 English possessions in France after the Treaty of Brétigny, 1360

B The Battle of Crécy, 1346

The Hundred Years War began in 1337, but the English were unable to do much against the French until 1346. In that year, Edward III took an army across the Channel. He had with him his eldest son, Edward, later known as the Black Prince, a boy of 16.

The army landed near Cherbourg. The King's plan was to march through Normandy to Flanders, doing as much damage as possible on the way. You can follow the route taken by the English, on the map below. As

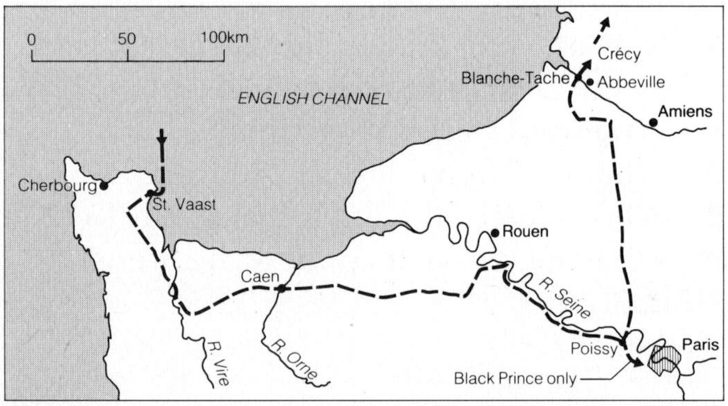

Figure 1 Edward III's march through Normandy

they went, they burnt towns and villages, and destroyed crops. They crossed the River Seine at Poissy, and the River Somme at the ford of Blanche-Tache. Shortly after that, they met an enormous French army at Crécy.

King Edward drew up his army in three divisions, or 'battles':

Document One

The King put his son, the Prince of Wales, in charge of the Vanguard. The Earls of Arundel and Northampton commanded the Main Battle. He took control of the Rearward Battle himself. He made sure that all his soldiers were ready for the enemy attack, and that the war horses were in the waggon park ready to chase the flying enemy. He then prayed to God and the Virgin Mary.

Our men made the day holy by fasting, and called on the Virgin Mary. They dug many holes in front of their lines, one foot deep and one foot wide. This was to make the French horses stumble.

The archers did not stand in front of the men-at-arms, and they did not meet the enemy face to face. Instead, they shot their arrows from the sides of the King's army.

Geoffrey le Baker, *Chronicle*

Note: 'men-at-arms' – knights, and others armed like them

1 What were the names of the three divisions of the English army?

2 Who had charge of each?

3 The English knights fought on foot. How can you tell?

4 How did the English try to make sure God was on their side?

5 What traps did they make for the French horses?

Figure 2 is a plan of the Battle of Crécy. Find the three 'battles' of the English army. Find the English archers. You can now see what Geoffrey le Baker meant about them. They are in a '**V**' and two half '**V**'s. As a result, they are not looking directly at the enemy, but across his front. This is so that they can deliver cross fire. Figure 3 will tell you about it.

The Rearward Battle, **3**, was the reserve. A good general does not put all his troops in the front line. Then, if the front line shows any sign of breaking, he has some men to give it support.

Here is what was happening on the French side. There were no fewer than three kings with their army. They were King Philip of France himself, and two of his allies, the blind King of Bohemia and the King of Majorca:

Document Two

The army of the French was divided into nine divisions. The vanguard was led by the King of Bohemia, a soldier of great experience. He had asked King Philip for the honour of leading the first division.

The French army was so large, that its leaders were sure they would win. They began to argue over which prisoners they should have. The King of Majorca wanted the King of England as his prize, others, the Earl of North-

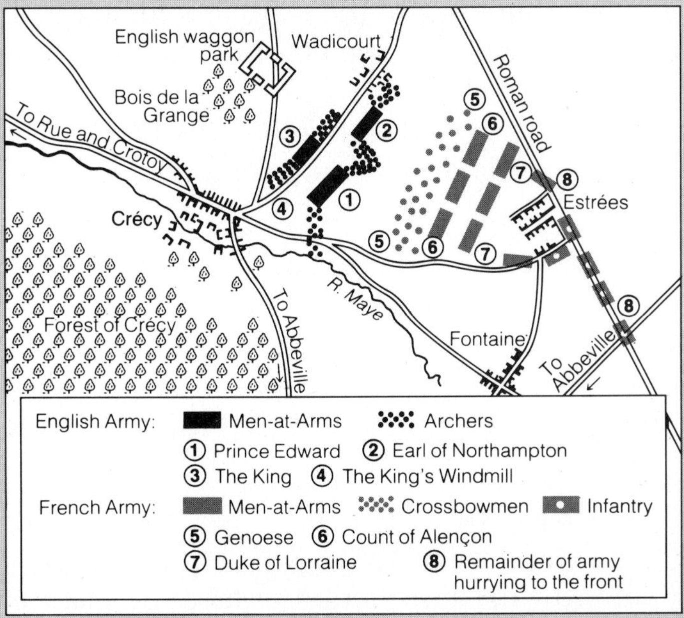

Figure 2
The Battle of Crécy

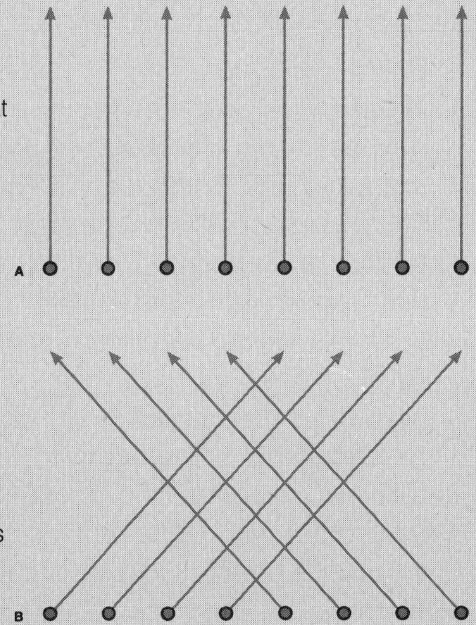

Figure 3
(right) Cross fire. At **A** each soldier is firing straight ahead at the man coming towards him. That means there are gaps between the lines of fire, in which an enemy may not be hit. But a good soldier fires at the enemy who is coming towards his friend, further down the line (**B**). The lines of fire cross, so the enemy soldiers are more likely to be hit.

ampton, and others wanted other leaders, depending on how important they were. But King Philip was afraid they might be busy capturing the English leaders, rather than trying to win the battle. He ordered the banner called the Oriflamme to be unfurled. When this was flying, it was unlawful for anyone, on pain of death, to spare a prisoner.
Geoffrey le Baker, *Chronicle*

1 How many divisions were there in the French army? Who led the vanguard?
2 Why were the French leaders sure they would win?
3 What did they argue about?
4 What was King Philip afraid they would do?
5 How did he try to prevent them?

For most of the day the two sides stood looking at each other. But the French army was growing stronger the whole time, as more and more men arrived. Then, at about three o'clock in the afternoon, the French attacked.

As you can see from the plan, the French had a force of crossbowmen in front of their army. These were men from Genoa, in northern Italy. They were sent forward to shoot gaps in the English lines, and so prepare the way for a cavalry charge.

Here is what happened:

Document Three
The first attack was made by the French against the English to the sound of trumpets, drums, kettle-drums and clarions. With a shout like thunder, the Genoese crossbowmen advanced. But none of their quarrels reached the English, falling a long way in front of them. When the Genoese crossbowmen raised their shout, the English archers were ordered to fire on them. They poured down arrows on their enemies, and ended the shower of quarrels with a hail of arrows.
Geoffrey le Baker, *Chronicle*

Note: 'quarrel' – arrow from a crossbow

1 What noises did the Genoese make before they attacked?
2 Why did they do this, do you suppose?
3 Why did the Genoese crossbowmen fail to hurt the English?
4 What happened when the English archers fired back?

The crossbow is a powerful, dangerous weapon. But it is impossible to fire it more than three times a minute. Look at page 7 to see how fast the English longbowmen could fire. This will explain why the Genoese crossbowmen were defeated.

This is how the battle continued:

Document Four
When they saw that their crossbowmen were not harming the English at all, the French men-at-arms rode down the crossbowmen. They crushed them beneath the feet of their horses, and charged headlong forward, to show the English how brave they were.

The Genoese who were being trampled gave such shrieks of pain that the men further behind in the French army thought it was the English who were being killed. They pressed forward, hard on the heels of those in front. But many of their horses were killed and wounded by the English archers, while others stumbled in the holes. Those who reached the English men-at-arms were beaten down with axes and swords. Meanwhile, in the middle of the host, many Frenchmen were crushed to death by the weight of numbers.
Geoffrey le Baker, *Chronicle*

1 What did the French men-at-arms do to their own crossbowmen?
2 Why did the men towards the rear of the French army think the English were being killed?
3 What did they do as a result?
4 What happened to the Frenchmen who reached the English men-at-arms?
5 Why were many men killed in the middle of the French army?

You will remember that Edward, the Black Prince had command of the English vanguard. Geoffrey le Baker describes how he fought:

Document Five
Edward, the King's eldest son, being then sixteen years old, showed his courage to the French. He pierced horses, laid low riders, shattered helmets, broke spears, parried blows aimed at him, helped his men, defended himself, helped to their feet friends who had fallen, and set all men a fine example.
Chronicle.

1 Describe some of the ways in which the Black Prince showed his skill and his courage.
2 What sort of education had the Black Prince received, do you suppose?

There is probably a great deal of truth in what Geoffrey le Baker said. But we must remember he was writing to please the King!

Here is what happened during the rest of the battle:

Document Six
The French kept changing their front line. They brought up fresh hordes to take the place of those who were killed, wounded or tired. These constant attacks kept the Prince and his companions fighting hard. The mass of the enemy was so great, that he was driven to fight on his knees. Then someone ran to the King, told him that his son was in danger, and begged for help. The King sent twenty knights. They found the Prince and his men leaning on their swords. They were taking breath and resting quietly on long mounds of corpses, waiting for the enemy, who had retired.

So the battle went on for most of the night. During this time, the French attacked fifteen times, but at last they fled in defeat.
Geoffrey le Baker, *Chronicle.*

1 Why did the Black Prince and his companions have a hard fight?
2 What help did the King send?
3 Was this help needed?
4 How many times did the French attack?
5 What did they do in the end?

Again, we must remember that Geoffrey le Baker was writing to please the King. He gives nearly all the credit to the Black Prince, and says almost nothing about the English archers. They prevented most of the French from reaching the English men-at-arms. Without the archers, the Black Prince and his companions must have been overpowered.

Crécy was a great victory for the English. Geoffrey le Baker tells us:

> *Document Seven*
> The number of French knights and nobles killed in this battle was more than 4000. No one troubled to count the others who were slain. The English King and his army gave thanks to God, rested themselves, and gathered their men together. They then discovered that only 40 of their army had been slain.
> *Chronicle*

According to Geoffrey le Baker:

1 How many French nobles and knights were killed?

2 How many of the English were killed?

We cannot be sure that Geoffrey le Baker's figures were at all accurate. But it is certain that the French lost more men at Crécy than the English did.

Figure 4 The Battle of Crécy. The English are on the right and the French are on the left.

The artist has shown several events in the one picture. At the front, Genoese crossbowmen are fighting English longbowmen. Which side has scored the most hits? In the battle, the range was much greater. But the artist could not have put both armies in, if he had shown the distance correctly.

Behind the crossbowmen who are firing, a French knight is striking another crossbowman. You will remember that the French rode down the Genoese when these failed in their attack (*Document Four*). Further back, French knights are running away.

C The Siege of Calais

After winning the Battle of Crécy, Edward III took his army to besiege Calais. Geoffrey le Baker tells us about the siege:

Document One

Calais is surrounded by a double wall and a double ditch. The King was unwilling to make an attack. He knew it would be too dangerous, because of the high walls and deep ditches. Moreover, he could not build siege engines, to destroy the walls. There was no firm ground on which to place them. Besides, even if the walls were down, the ditches were deep and the tide filled them twice a day. Therefore the King neither attacked nor bombarded the walls. Instead, he relied on hunger, which enters closed doors, to conquer the town.

Chronicle

1 How was Calais defended?
2 Why did the English not attack the town?
3 Why did they not bombard it with siege engines?
4 How did they hope to capture it?

This was how the English tried to prevent the French from sending supplies to Calais by sea:

Document Two

The king kept a great fleet to besiege the town, and did not allow it to leave. At different times, the Normandy pirates captured 15 of his ships. Some they kept, others they burnt.

From the shore to deep water was a stretch where the men of Boulogne tried to bring supplies to Calais. They used small boats which kept close to the shore. Here, the Earl of Northampton made a fence of stakes to stop these small boats. From time to time, the French Admiral attacked the English ships with his fleet. This was to give the small ships the chance to bring in supplies. But the Earl of Northampton prevented him.

Geoffrey le Baker, *Chronicle*

1 Which pirates attacked the English fleet? What did they succeed in doing?
2 How did the men of Boulogne try to bring in supplies?
3 How did the Earl of Northampton prevent them?

After several months, the Governor of Calais wrote a letter to the King of France. He gave it to the captain of a ship that had managed to steal into the harbour. On her way out, the ship was captured by the English. The captain just had time to tie the letter to an axe head, and throw it overboard. However, the English found it at low tide. This is what it said:

Document Three

Know most dread and dear Lord that the town has great need of corn, wine and meal.

Everything is eaten – dogs, cats, horses – and we have nothing to live on, unless we eat each other. We have therefore agreed that if help does not come at once, to sally out into the open and fight for life or death. For we would rather die with honour on the field than eat each other. I beg you to help us, for unless you do so soon the town will be lost with every soul in it.

Robert de Avesbury, *Chronicle*

1 What do the people of Calais need?
2 What have they been eating?
3 What is the only thing left to eat?
4 What have they decided to do, if help does not arrive?

The English were suffereing as well.' Winter came, and since their horses had no shelter, many died of the cold. Men were dying too, from disease. The King was desperate for reinforcements. He even offered pardons to murderers and criminals, if they would join his army in France. The English nobles sent for men, including the Black Prince. You will remember he was Prince of Wales. He ordered his officials to send him 1200 Welshmen, half of them armed with lances, and half of them archers. Any who refused to join the army were to be arrested. The Prince also demanded large sums of money.

Figure 1 The message is thrown overboard

Geoffrey le Baker says:

Document Four

The siege went on from the Feast of the Nativity of the Virgin (September 4th), through the whole winter and much of the summer. Then, on the Monday before the Feast of St. John (June 25th), the French King arrived. He swore that he would raise the siege, either by war or peace.

First of all, the King of France sent his messengers, the Counts of Bourbon and Armagnac. They met the Duke of Lancaster and the Earl of Northampton, and tried to arrange a truce. But the English would not agree. So, after warlike tournaments, both sides went back to their camps.

On the second day, the King of France suggested a day for a battle. This, the King of England accepted.

Meanwhile, the people of Calais sent the King of France signs to tell him they were in serious trouble. Shortly after dark, they made a great light on top of one of their highest towers. They also made a great shout and noise with trumpets and drums. The second night they did the same, but rather less. The third night they made a very small fire, and gave a sorrowful cry. That way, they showed that they no longer had the strength to defend the town.

At last, the day of the battle drew near. But King Edward had reinforcements of 17000 troops. When the French King saw this, he fled. On leaving, he set fire to his tents, as a sign to the people of the town that he could not help them.

Chronicle

1 How many months was it before the French King arrived to help Calais?

2 What did the King of France try to arrange when he first arrived?
3 What agreement did he make with the King of England on the second day?
4 What message did the people of Calais want to send to the King?
5 Describe, in your own words, how they sent their message.
6 Why did the French King run away, rather than give battle?
7 How did he let the people of Calais know he could not help them?
8 Documents Three and Four show how difficult it could be to send messages in time of war. How do armies send messages to each other today?

Geoffrey le Baker goes on:

Document Five

When the defenders of Calais saw that their King had left, they took down their flag, and threw it from the tower into the ditch. Then John de Vienne, their captain, came out to the King of England. He was riding a little nag, because he was lame, and he had a halter round his neck. Other soldiers and burgesses followed him on foot, bare-headed and bare-footed. They, too had halters around their necks.

Then John de Vienne gave the King a warlike sword, as a sign of surrender. Next, he handed him the keys of the town. Thirdly, he begged for mercy, and delivered him the sword of peace.

The King accepted what was offered him, and sent the captain with fifteen burgesses and as many knights, into England, enriching them with valuable gifts. As for the common people of the town, he first gave them food, and then ordered them to be taken safely to Guines.

Chronicle

Notes: 'halter' – hangman's rope. The men wore the ropes to show they were willing to die for their fellow townsmen.
'burgess' – important citizen
Guines was a town that was still in French hands.

Figure 2 (right) The Siege of Calais

1 What did the people of Calais do when the French King fled?
2 Why did they not come out and fight, as they had said they would, do you think?
3 What men came out to surrender the town? How were they dressed?
4 What three things did they give the King? What did they ask him?
5 What happened to some of the important citizens and soldiers?
6 What happened to the common people?

It might sound as if Edward III was being kind to the ordinary people of Calais. In fact, he was driving them from their homes, to make room for settlers from England.

There is another story of the surrender of Calais, written by a chronicler called Froissart. He says the King was going to execute six of the burgesses, but then this happened:

Document Six

The noble Queen of England wept bitterly. She flung herself on her knees before her lord the King and said, 'Dear sir, since I came here from across the sea I have not asked you for anything. Now I beg you that for the sake of the Son and Blessed Mary, and for love of me, that you will have mercy on these six men.'

The King hesitated and looked at the good lady his wife, on her knees before him and in tears. His heart softened and he said, 'Madam, I wish you were not here. You pray so earnestly that I dare not refuse the gift you ask. Though I am very unwilling, I grant it to you.'

The brave lady answered, 'My lord, many thanks!' She told the six burgesses to stand and took the ropes from their necks. Then she led them to her hostel, and gave them clothes and food and made them comfortable that day. And in the morning, she gave them money, and told two knights to lead them away from the army, as far as they could, until they were out of danger.

Chronicles

D The Battle of Poitiers

In 1356, the Black Prince led a raid deep into France. Near Poitiers he was caught by a large French army commanded by the French King, John II. The Black Prince had to stand and fight, though he was heavily outnumbered.

The English took up their position on a hill. Their army was in three divisions, known as 'battles'. The Prince put two of his battles in the front line. The third, which was his own, he kept in reserve. Find the English army on the map (Figure 1).

At the head of the French army there were some mounted knights. They hoped to ride down the English archers, so making way for the main attacks which were to follow. The rest of the French army was in three battles, one behind the other. All the men in these battles were dismounted. It seems that the French had learnt some lessons from Crécy. They were going to make just one attack on horseback. The others would be on foot.

Figure 1 The Battle of Poitiers

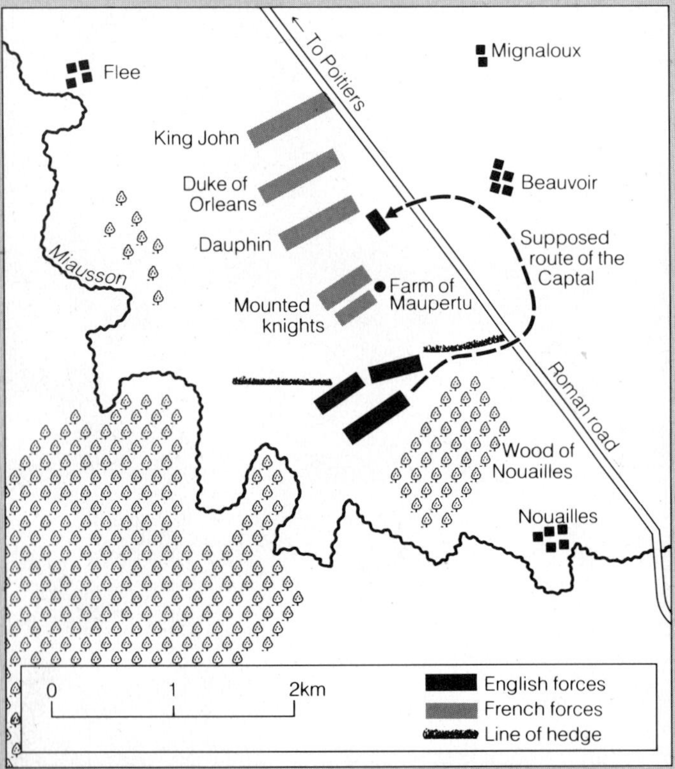

This is what happened when the French cavalry attacked:

Document One

At first, our archers had little success. The French horsemen were well protected by their plate armour, so that the arrows either fell to the ground, or glanced up to the sky. When he saw this, the Earl of Warwick ordered his archers to move to one side, where they could shoot at the legs of the horses. When this was done, some of the wounded horses reared up, and those who sat on them fell off. Other horses turned tail and ran against those that followed them, causing great destruction.
Geoffrey le Baker, *Chronicle*

1 Why did the English archers have little success, at first?

2 What did the Earl of Warwick order them to do? What happened then?

This is what happened next:

Document Two

Now the first of the French dismounted battles attacked. It was led by the eldest son of the French King, the Dauphin. The soldiers in this army were more dreadful and fierce than those that had been driven off before. But they did not frighten our men. Both sides fought bravely, and shouts of 'St. George!' and 'St. Denis!' rose to the skies. Some of our men wore out their weapons, so they took spears and swords from Frenchmen they had slain. Our archers tore arrows from wretches who were only half dead. All of our men were either wounded, or worn out by hard labour.
Geoffrey le Baker, *Chronicle*

1 Who led this attack on the English?

2 What shows that the English had to fight very hard?

At last, the Dauphin's men fled from the field. But the English were nearly exhausted, and the French still had two battles they had not used. However, the French in the second battle, under the Duke of Orleans, ran away

Figure 2 The Battle of Poitiers. English archers are wounding the French horses. Some arrows are also piercing the armour of the French knights. Read *Document One* to see if this really happened.

without fighting. King John now led the last battle into the attack:

Document Three

The air was filled with arrows shot by the English archers. But the French were in a solid mass and they protected themselves by shields held close together. Our archers emptied their quivers in vain. Then, having no more than swords and small shields, they had to fight hand to hand with French knights in full armour.

Meanwhile, the Captal de Buch hurried down a side track with a small force. He worked his way to the rear of the French army, and burst upon them. At the same time, our brave Prince charged the French from the front. The unhappy French, attacked on both sides, were thrown into confusion. Their banners began to totter, and dying men fell on each other. The Prince of Wales cut through their ranks, fighting like a lion, and took the King of France prisoner.

Geoffrey le Baker, *Chronicle*

Note: The Captal de Buch was a Gascon officer.

1 Why were the English archers unable to kill many of the French?

2 From which direction did the Captal de Buch attack the French?

3 What was the result of his attack?

The battle of Poitiers shows that archers were not bound to have their own way. Men-at-arms could do well against them, if they fought properly. At Poitiers the English were very lucky to win. They were saved only by the cowardice of the Duke of Orleans' men, and by the Captal de Buch's attack on the French rear.

E Chevauchées

When an English army invaded France, its leaders were not expecting to defeat the French army in a big battle. Indeed, a battle was one thing they hoped to avoid. What they wanted to do was go on a 'chevauchée'. The word 'chevauchée' means 'ride'. It was a polite word for a journey in which the army would destroy everything it could find. The idea was to cause so much damage and suffering that the people of France would want to surrender. The British and the Germans tried much the same thing in the Second World War. They bombed each others cities from the air.

Here are some descriptions of chevauchées:

Document One

a. We made our way through the land of Toulouse. We burnt and destroyed many fine towns, for the land was very rich. No day passed without our army taking some town or fortress.
Letter of the Black Prince, 1355

b. When they entered a fertile area, they sent their scouts to strip the land of food. Often they

Figure 1 Some of the chevauchées made during the war

Figure 2 Army on the march

Figure 3 Soldiers looting a house. What are the men taking from the house? What are they doing, as well as stealing from the house?

did so for thirty miles on both sides. If there was plenty of food, they stayed two or three days, bringing many cattle back to the army. They found a lot of wine, more than they needed, and they wasted much of it.
Froissart, *Chronicles*

1 According to the Black Prince, what places did his men capture and destroy? (In fact, the English usually left strongly defended places alone. Instead, they destroyed villages and farms.)

2 According to Froissart:
i. How wide an area did the English plunder?
ii. How long would they stay in an area?
iii. What happened to much of the wine that they took?

Here are some descriptions of the French countryside, after English chevauchées:

Document Two

a. From the Loire to the Seine, the peasants have been slain or put to flight. I have seen vast plains quite deserted, uncultivated, empty of inhabitants, covered with bushes and brambles. Indeed, in some districts, dense forests are starting to grow.
Thomas Basin, *Histoire de Charles VII*

Figure 4 Gateway to Issoudun. The English burnt the suburbs of this town in 1356. But they could not touch the town itself, because it had strong defences. Some of these are still standing today, as you can see.

b. There were no cattle in the fields. No cock crowed in the night. Rabbits and hares played freely in the deserted fields, for no-one dared go hunting. No travellers went along the roads, carrying their cheese and butter to market. Houses and churches were smoking ruins. Men were no longer made happy by the sight of fields full of growing grain. Instead, they were saddened by nettles and thistles springing up everywhere. The pleasant sound of the bell was still heard, but not to call people to prayer. It was a warning that the enemy was coming.
Jean de Venette, *Chronicle*

1 What was growing in the fields?
2 What has happened to the farm animals?
3 What has happened to the buildings?

In 1422 a citizen of Paris wrote:

Document Three
At this time, the English were all over Brie, plundering everywhere. Often, complaints were made to the English lords, but they only laughed and egged on their troops worse than before. Hence, most of the peasants gave up trying to work or to sow their fields. In their despair they even left their families. They said to each other, 'What shall we do? Let us put everything into the hands of the devil. We may as well do our worst, as do our best, so let us do the worst we can. We have to leave our wives and children and flee to the woods like wandering beasts.'
Journal d'un bourgeois de Paris

1 What were the English doing in Brie?
2 What happened when the people complained to the English lords?
3 What did the peasants give up doing?
4 What did they do with their families?

Here is a letter written by the prior of a French monastery:

Document Four
The English came to Chantecocq, and set fire to almost the whole countryside. They then brought the entire region under their rule. They ordered the people who were at all wealthy to pay ransom. If they did not, their goods would be seized, their houses burnt, and they themselves would be killed. Terrified by this, many people promised to give the English money and flour, oats and other food, if only they would leave them alone. They were killing many men. Some they kept in prison, threatening them with death. Some they tortured without mercy.

Other people, wanting to escape, made huts in the woods. There they ate their bit of bread in fear and sorrow. I was among them for I had built a hut in the wood of Cauda. Here I stayed with many of my neighbours. Daily, we heard about the horrible deeds of our enemies. They burnt houses, and left many dead bodies lying about the villages, as is their vile custom. One night those cursed English found my hut. They nearly took me as I slept, but by the grace of God, I managed to run away. Naked as I was, I

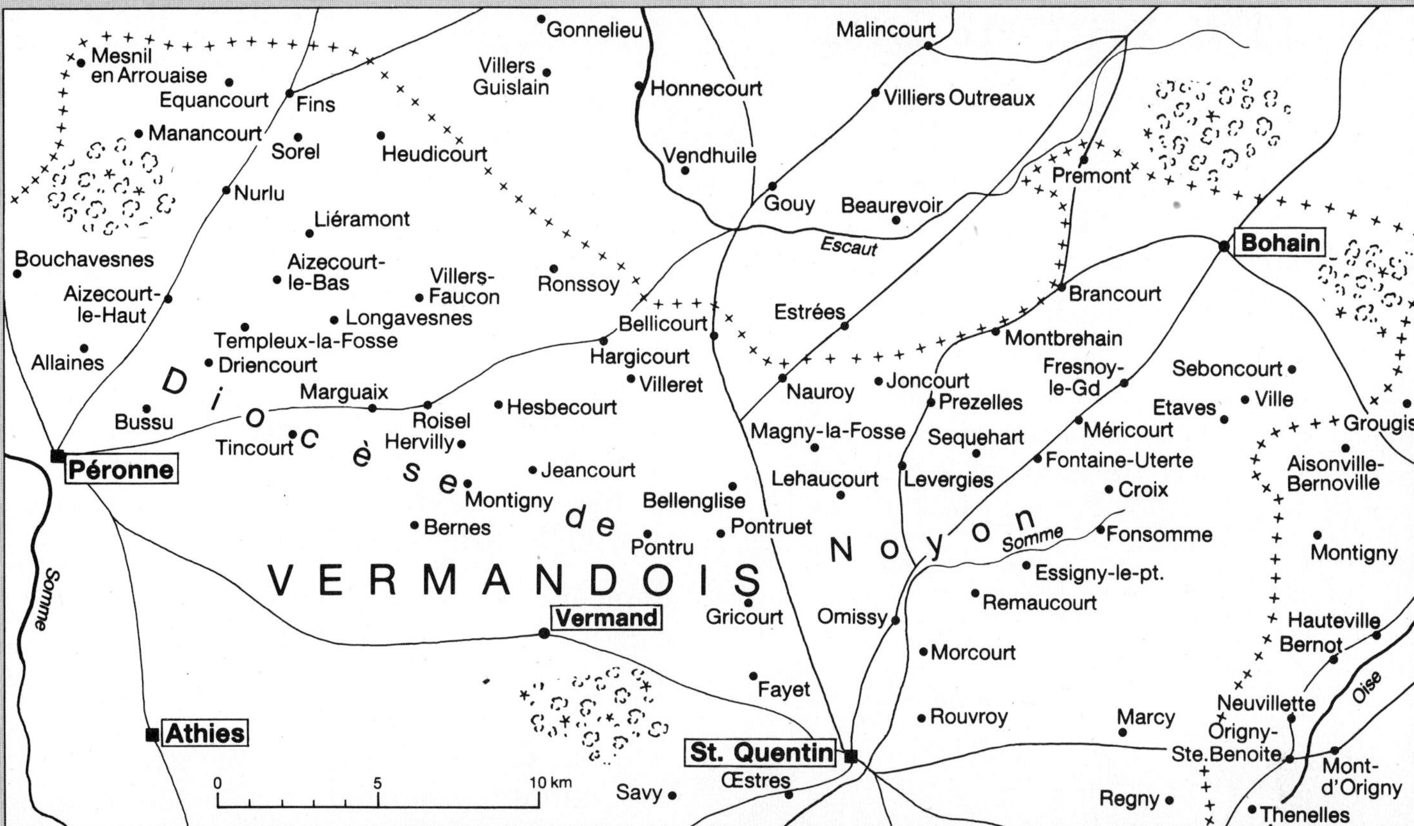

Figure 5 Part of Cambrai, a devastated area in Northern France. The villages shown on the map were all destroyed by the English in 1340. Estimate how many there were in this small area. Many of the towns were not destroyed; their names are shown in rectangles. Why did the English leave them alone, do you suppose? (See caption to Figure 4.)

escaped, taking with me only my tunic and my hood. I crossed the marsh, and stayed there, trembling with fear, and shivering with cold. I remained long enough to see my hut completely destroyed.

Later, I came to an agreement with the English, and returned to my monastery. But they spoiled all the furniture in my house, drank four casks of wine, carried off a peck of oats, took all my clothes, stole the horses and killed all my pigeons.

Tribulations d'un religieux

1 What did the English do when they arrived?
2 What did they order the wealthier people to do?
3 How did they ill-treat some of the people?
4 Where did some of the people go to escape?
5 Describe, in your own words, how the prior escaped from the English.
6 How did the English ill-treat the prior, even after he had made an agreement with them?

Once in a while, French civilians managed to get their hands on English soldiers. In 1437 the French army took a fortress. The English garrison of 240 surrendered on condition their lives were spared. But this is what happened:

Document Five

The English were taken some six miles away by two French knights, who could hardly protect them. All who could get near killed them with sticks and stones, like dogs. The two knights did their best until Châteauneuf de Quintin. Here, butchers, carpenters and others came out and put the English to death like sheep. The people of Châteauneuf de Quintin carried the corpses to quarries and ditches outside the town, where they were eaten by dogs and birds.

Grandes Chroniques

3 The War at Sea

A Ships

No ships have survived from the Middle Ages, but we do have a good idea of what they looked like. For one thing, seaside towns usually put pictures of ships on their seals. Figure 1 shows the seal of Winchelsea of about 1340.

Figure 1 Seal of Winchelsea, about 1340

Probably, the first thing that you will notice about this ship, is that it is very small. You are quite right to think so, but, up to a point, the seal is misleading. The problem is, that artists of the Middle Ages usually drew people much larger than they were. The men shown here are, perhaps, four or five times as big as they should be. From this, you can work out, very roughly, the size of the ship:

1 Mark the height of a man on the edge of a piece of scrap paper. You will have to guess a little, as you cannot see anyone's feet. (Probably, the figure climbing the rigging is a boy.)
2 Using your mark as a ruler, see how many men, lying head to toe, would reach the length of the ship.
3 Multiply this figure by 1.7 metres, to give you the length of the ship as the artist has drawn it.
4 Multiply this figure by four or five to give you the true length of the ship.

Compare the length of the ship with the length of you garden, or the length of a football pitch. You will realise that the ship of the Middle Ages was much bigger than the Winchelsea seal suggests. At the same time, it was minute compared with modern ships. The medieval ship would have been 150 or 200 tonnes. What is the tonnage of the largest ship afloat today? (You will find the answer in the *Guinness Book of Records*.)

Today, we have merchant ships and warships, and they are quite different from each other. That was not true of England in the Middle Ages. All ships were merchant ships, and in time of war, the king took as many as he needed. He then turned them into warships by having castles built on them. Find these castles in Figure 1. Where are they placed on the ship? When the king had finished with a ship, he gave it back to its owners. The castles were then taken down.

How many masts are there on the ship in Figure 1? How many sails are there? At present, the sail is furled. The boy climbing the rigging is probably going to let it down. If he had already done so, you would be able to see that it is roughly square in shape.

A square sail is very good, when the wind is behind the ship. But a medieval ship could not sail into the wind, as a modern yacht can. A modern yacht can put to sea, whatever the direction of the wind. A ship of the Middle

Figure 2 Model of a ship of about 1430

Ages had to wait until the wind was in the right direction.

The Winchelsea ship does not have a rudder. Instead, there is a steering oar fitted to one side. Find it on the picture. Such an oar is not as good as a stern rudder.

Now look at Figure 3. Ships like this were built in about 1430, which is a hundred years later than the one on the Winchelsea seal.

There have been a few changes. For example, the castles are now built as part of the hull, so they cannot be taken down. A big improvement is the rudder, which will make the ship easier to steer. Also, this ship is likely to be bigger. Probably, it was between 250 and 300 tonnes. But it still has just the one square sail. It can only put to sea if the wind is right.

This model shows how broad ships were. Many were only three times as long as they were wide. You can see, too that the bows and stern are rounded, instead of coming to a fine point. The ship is very like a floating shoe box. That means, it can carry plenty of cargo. But it also means it is slow, which is a disadvantage for a warship.

The model has a 'fighting top' on its mast. From here, men could shoot arrows and hurl spears and stones at their enemies. Fighting tops were not new. The Winchelsea ship might well have had one, but it has not been drawn.

Here now is a description of a sea battle:

Document One

An iron shower of quarrels from crossbows and arrows from long bows brought death to thousands of men. Those who wished or dared to do so fought hand to hand with spears, battle axes and swords. Stones hurled from the tops of masts dashed out the brains of many.
Geoffrey le Baker, *Chronicle*

1 What weapons are being used?
2 Would any of these weapons sink a ship?
3 How far apart were the ships, as they fought with each other, do you think? Given reasons for your answer.

B The Battle of Sluys

In 1340 there was a great sea battle between the English, under Edward III, and the French. It took place at Sluys, on the coast of the Netherlands.

The French had many of their own ships, and they had been joined by others, belonging to their allies, the Spaniards. There were also some vessels from Genoa, whose crews were in the pay of the French. English spies reported that they had seen 'so great a number of ships that their masts seemed to be like a forest'. None the less, Edward III decided to attack. Jean Froissart describes the battle:

Document One

King Edward sent his largest ships first, full of archers. Between every two ships of archers he had one ship with men-at-arms. Then he made another squadron, to stay in the rear, as a reserve.

When the King and his marshals had drawn up the battle line, he ordered the fleet to turn a little so that the sun was not in his men's eyes. And when the French saw them retire, they wondered why they did so. Some said, 'They have decided to leave us alone, and will go back home.' Then they put their fleet in battle order, for they were good seamen. They put the *Christopher,* which they had captured from the English tne year before, to the front, filled with crossbowmen. Then they sounded their trumpets and attacked their enemies.

Chronicles

1 Draw a sketch plan to show how Edward III arranged his ships for battle.
2 Compare this with the way he arranged his army forthe Battle of Crécy. (See page 14.)
3 What ship had the French captured from the English?

Figure 1 Sea battle. What weapons are the soldiers using? The soldier on the right of the picture, near the front, has a hook in his hand. What is he doing with it? (See *Document Two*.)

4 Where did the French place this ship? What men were in her?
5 Compare this arrangement with the one the French made at the start of the Battle of Crécy.

Your answers to these questions should show you that a battle at sea was, in some ways, like a battle on land.

Jean Froissart tells us about the fighting:

Document Two
Then began a fierce battle. The archers and crossbowmen fired their arrows, while the men-at-arms fought hand to hand. So that they could do so more easily, they had great hooks of iron, to throw out of one ship into another and so tie them fast together.

There were many brave deeds done and, at last, the great *Christopher* was captured by the English. They put archers into her and took her to fight the Genoese.

The battle was fierce and terrible, for battles at sea are more dangerous than battles on land. At sea, there is no retreating, or running away. The only thing to do is to fight as bravely as possible.

The battle lasted from morning to noon, and the English had great difficulty, for their enemies outnumbered them by four to one. The King of England was himself a noble knight, and so were many other noble lords. They fought so well that they won the victory. The Frenchmen and their allies were either slain or drowned. Not one escaped.
Chronicles

1 How did the men-at-arms fight?
2 What was done to make this possible? (Again, you can see that a battle at sea was very like a battle on land.)
3 What ship did the English capture?
4 What did they do with her?
5 Why are battles at sea more dangerous than battles on land?
6 How many times were the English outnumbered?
7 Why did they win, in spite of that?

Figure 2 Sea battle. What weapons are the soldiers using? How can you tell that this picture was drawn later than Figure 1? (Look at the castles on the ships.)

8 How many of the French and their allies escaped?

Froissart tells us a lot about the Battle of Sluys, but there is a puzzle. He says that the English were outnumbered by four to one. If that was so, how did they manage to win? Froissart says it was because they fought so well, but that could not be the whole of the answer. There are a number of questions we could ask:

1 Was Froissart wrong?
2 Did the English have some advantages which Froissart does not mention?
3 Did the French make some mistakes which Froissart does not mention?

Another puzzle in Froissart's account is the remark that not a single one of the men on the French side escaped. Do you think that is likely?

Figure 3 The Battle of Sluys

Here are some extracts from another chronicle:

Document Three

a. When King Edward saw his enemies, it was a most dreadful thing to behold, for the fleet of France was strongly bound together with massive chains and bars.

b. And then did our King, with 300 ships, vigorously attack the French with their 500 great ships. Our archers began to fire as densely as hail falls in winter, so that the French did not dare look up, or hold up their heads.

Chronicles of London

1 By how much did the French outnumber the English?

2 How fast did the English archers fire their arrows? Do you think this is a good description of English longbowmen in action? (Look back to page 7.)

3 What had the French done with their ships?

This chronicle then, seems to give us some of the answers to our questions:

1 The English were not outnumbered by nearly as much as Froissart says.

2 The English had a big advantage with their longbowmen, just as they did in the battles on land.

3 The French wanted to prevent the English breaking through their fleet, so they chained their ships together. That meant it was impossible to manoeuvre them, which was a serious disadvantage.

Here now is part of Geoffrey le Baker's account of Sluys:

Document Four

The French fleet, divided into three squadrons, moved forward a mile towards the English fleet. When they saw this, the King of England and his men ran to arms and were soon ready. After nine o'clock, the English had the wind and the sun behind them and the flow of the tide with them, and so they attacked.

After a hard struggle, the French in the first squadron were defeated, and the English seized their ships.

The English then attacked the second squadron. This was more easily defeated than the first, because most of the French leapt overboard without fighting.

The first and second squadrons of ships were thus captured. But dusk was falling, and the English decided to wait until morning. The night was dark, and they were weary. During the night, 30 ships of the third squadron fled.

Chronicle

1 Into how many squadrons did the French divide their fleet?

2 What three things did the English have in their favour, after nine o'clock?

3 Which part of the French fleet did the English attack, at first?

4 Which part of the French fleet did the English attack next?

5 Why did the English not make a third attack?

6 What happened in the night?

7 Did the English attack the whole of the French fleet, at any one time?

You can see that Geoffrey le Baker's chronicle gives us some more answers to our problems. The English not only had the advantage of their longbows. The wind and the tide were behind them. That meant they were able to attack just one third of the French fleet at a time. The French ships that were not in the fight should, of course, have come to the aid of their friends. This they could not do. For one thing, the wind and the tide were against them. For another, they were chained together, so that it was very difficult for them to move.

Now pretend you were an English archer at Sluys. Describe the battle, and explain why the English won.

C Raids on the Coast

Winning the Battle of Sluys did not mean that the English had won the war at sea. From time to time they lost battles. For example, in 1372, an English fleet under the Earl of Pembroke met a Spanish fleet off La Rochelle. The Spaniards thoroughly defeated the English. Pembroke lost most of his ships and was himself taken prisoner.

Big battles like Sluys and La Rochelle did not happen very often, but the French and the Spaniards carried out many raids on the coast of England. Here is a description of one:

Document One
At this time (1360), French and Norman knights, some 3000 fighting men, made an expedition to England. They meant to stay there, so as to make the King of England leave France, in order to save his own country.

The Frenchmen arrived in Winchelsea, remained in the town a day and a night, and set fire to it on leaving. They lost two ships which ran aground, and about 300 men who were slain by the people who attacked them.
Sir Thomas Gray, *Scalacronica*

1 How many French and Normans invaded England?
2 What did they hope to make the King of England do?
3 Which town did they attack? How long did they stay in it? What did they do to it before they left?
4 How many ships and men did they lose?

The English accounts usually make it sound as if the French raids were not very successful. In fact, they often did a lot of damage. For example, in 1338 the French completely destroyed Southampton. At times, even the people of London were worried:

Document Two
In 1385 a proclamation was made to say that those able and willing to go to the sea coast in defence of the City should come to the Guildhall. There they would receive their pay, namely 12 pence a day for men-at-arms and 6 pence a day for archers. Also, that those men-at-arms and archers who were able, but not willing to go, should be arrested as traitors.
London Letter Book H

1 What are the men who are able to defend the City to do?
2 What will happen to those who refuse?

Figure 1 Fowey, Cornwall. Fowey was an important port in the Middle Ages. In 1346 it sent 47 ships to help Edward III blockade Calais. The town was the home of a band of pirates called the 'Fowey Gallants'. They often raided the coast of France. Sometimes, the French raided Fowey in return.

Figure 2 (right) The French burn Winchelsea

Sometimes the English attacked the coast of France. Here is an example of a pair of 'tit for tat' raids. First of all, this is what the French did:

Document Three
The Bretons and the French came to Plymouth with a big fleet. They burst in by night, burnt the town and plundered the whole night, until 3 o'clock the next day. No one came to help. This disaster was the result of the stupidity and pride of the townsmen, who refused help from their neighbours. For when the enemy fleet was seen, the country people ran to the town, to defend it. But the people of Plymouth at once doubled the price of food in the town.

When the country people asked why they did it, they said they had no need of help, and could manage on their own. When they heard this rude answer, the people who had come to help went away. And so the French were able to rob the town quite easily, and quietly took to their ships whatever they wanted.
Thomas Walsingham, *Annals of Henry IV*

1 How long were the French in Plymouth?
2 What did the country folk do when they saw the French fleet?
3 How did the people of Plymouth make them leave?
4 What reason did they give for doing this?
5 What happened as a result?

Here is the revenge the English took:

Document Four
William de Wilford, with sailors from Dartmouth, Bristol and Plymouth, sailed to Brittany. He took six ships near the fortress of Brest. The next day, he and his men took four ships laden with iron, oil and tallow. When this was done, they crossed to Belle Isle, where they took thirty vessels. These were filled with wine to the number of 1000 casks. Leaving there, 4000 of his men landed at Penare, and burnt farms and manor houses. They went inland six leagues. On their return to the sea, they burnt 40 vessels great and small. The village of St. Matthew was also burnt to the ground. So they came home, bearing joyful news to their own country, and leaving Brittany sad.
Thomas Walsingham, *Annals of Henry IV*

Note: 'tallow' – animal fat used for making candles

1 How many ships did the English capture or destroy?
2 What cargoes did they capture?
3 What damage did they do on land?

4 War with Scotland

A Border Raids between England and Scotland

The English and the Scots were old enemies. The folk who lived either side of the border often raided each other. Also, the Scots took advantage of the Hundred Years War to make serious attacks on England.

Jean Froissart describes the Scots:

Document One

The Scottish men are right hardy, and good travellers in armour and in war. For when they come into England, they will drive their whole army 24 miles in a single day. They are all on horseback. The knights and squires are well horsed, and the ordinary soldiers ride ponies.

Figure 1 Map of Cumberland, showing villages destroyed by the Scots. Similar maps could be drawn of all the counties, on both sides of the border.

They bring with them no carts, because of the mountains they have to cross.

They take with them no bread or wine. During a war they will live for a long time on half-cooked meat, with nothing to drink but water from the rivers. Nor do they carry any pots or pans, since they cook animals in their skins.

They are sure to find plenty of cattle in the lands they travel through. Also, behind his saddle, each man carries a broad metal plate and a little sack, full of oatmeal. After they have eaten their meat, they put this plate on the fire, and mix some oatmeal with water. When the plate is hot, they drop a little of the thin paste on it. That way, they make a small cake, like a biscuit.

Chronicles

1 How far can the Scottish army go in a day?
2 Why is this possible?
3 What do the Scots eat and drink?
4 How do they manage without pots and pans?
5 How do they cook their oatmeal?
6 Do you have a flat iron plate like the ones mentioned here, in your kitchen? If so, what do you call it, and what do you cook on it?

Here are descriptions of a Scottish raid made in 1388:

Document Two

a. On 29 June the Scots invaded England with two armies, one in the east and the other in the west. They burnt and plundered the entire countryside as far as Tynemouth. The ordinary people they captured, they killed savagely; more than 400 wealthy men were taken prisoner. In the middle of July they returned, unresisted, to Scotland. They took

Figure 2 An English army invades Scotland. The English are on the right. The Scots are on the left, most of them on the hill. The artist has drawn several events in the same picture. Try to decide what is happening in different parts of the picture.

with them enormous plunder.
Westminster Chronicle

b. Both killing and burning they committed many cruelties against infants and pregnant women. Near Gilsland they locked 200 or more weak old men in their houses, and without mercy, burned them to death.
Henry Knighton, *Chronicle*

1 How long were the Scots in England?
2 Describe some of the things they did.
3 How did they treat wealthy people differently from ordinary people? Why was that, do you suppose?

In 1385 some French soldiers came to help the Scots. The English king, Richard II, decided to attack Scotland. Here is an account of the raid:

Document Three
Accompanied by a large army and with his banner unfurled, the King of England entered Scotland. That night the king made camp with his army in the Forest of Ettrick. There he put to death all the Scots and Frenchmen he was able to capture.

They then marched on for a week towards Melrose Abbey, killing, plundering and burning along a six-mile front. They left the entire countryside in ruins behind them. Since Melrose Abbey had sheltered their enemies, they burnt it. From there as far as the Firth of Forth, they laid waste the whole of Lothian and reduced Newbattle Abbey to dust. Always, their enemies fled before them.

On 11 August, the King reached Edinburgh, the capital of Scotland. He ordered it to be destroyed by fire, together with Holyrood Abbey, which is close by.
Westminster Chronicle

Note: Usually, soldiers did not attack sacred buildings like churches and monasteries. They wanted God to be on their side!

1 Describe some of the things the English did in Scotland.
2 Do you think they were any better, or any worse than the Scots?

B The Battle of Otterburn, 1388

Otterburn was the most important battle between the English and the Scots during the period of the Hundred Years War.

The Scots invaded England, and an English army marched against them. It was led by the two sons of the Earl of Northumberland, Sir Henry and Sir Ralph Percy. There was also a second English army in the field. It was led by the Bishop of Durham.

Soon, a small group of English knights found the Scottish army. It was at Otterburn, a village about thirty miles northwest of Newcastle-on-Tyne. The knights reported to Sir Henry and Sir Ralph Percy:

Document One

'The Scots are at Otterburn. And Sirs, their main army is not with them, for there are no more than 3000 of them'

When Sir Henry heard that, he was full of joy. He said, 'Sirs, let us leap on our horses. By the faith that I owe to God and to my father, we will go and fight with them this very night.'

The Bishop of Durham had heard that the Scots were at Newcastle, and was on his way with a large army. But Sir Henry Percy would not wait. He had 600 knights and 8000 foot soldiers. He thought that was enough to fight the Scots, who had only 300 knights and 3000 foot soldiers.

Froissart, *Chronicles*

1 What news did the knights bring?
2 What did Sir Henry Percy decide to do when he heard this news?
3 Who was on his way to help the English?
4 Why did Sir Henry Percy not wait for him?
5 Froissart gives two different figures for the size of the Scottish army. What are they?

The English were six miles from the Scottish camp, and night had fallen before they arrived. But there was a full moon, and they attacked at once. In Document Two Froissart describes what happened:

Figure 1 Site of the Battle of Otterburn. No-one is sure where exactly the battle was fought, but it is said that the Scottish army was on this hillside.

Document Two

I was told by men who were there, that this battle was as fierce as any that have been fought. I can believe it, for the English and the Scots are good men of war. When they meet, there is a hard fight, which goes on for as long as spears, swords, axes and daggers will last.

At first, the English were so many that they drove back their enemies. Then the leader of the Scots, the brave Earl Douglas, took his axe in both hands. He went into the thick of the battle and fought so well that no-one dared go near him. But at last he was wounded by three spears, all at once. One struck him on the shoulder. Another struck him on the chest, and glanced down to his belly. The third struck him in the thigh. All three wounds were serious, so he fell to the ground. He was then hit on the head with an axe, and was wounded again in the thigh.

The English knew they had knocked some-one down, but they were not aware who it was. Had they known, they would probably have been so encouraged that they would have won the battle.

Chronicles

1 According to Froissart, why was the battle very fierce?

Figure 2 Knights fighting hand-to-hand. The Battle of Otterburn would have been like this.

2 What did the English manage to do, at first?
3 What did Earl Douglas do, when he saw what was happening?
4 How many times was Douglas wounded?
5 What might have happened if the English had known that it was Douglas they had knocked down?

Froissart tells us what happened next:

Document Three
Douglas's men had followed him as closely as they could, and several knights came to him. Sir John Sinclair asked him how he was. 'I am dying.' he said. 'But I thank God that I do so like my ancestors. Few of them died in their beds. But I beg of you, take up my banner, and revenge me.'

The knights did as the Earl had asked. They picked up his banner and shouted, 'Douglas!' The men behind heard the cry. They gathered round the banner and attacked the English so bravely that they fled. The chase lasted for five miles. If the Scots had had enough men, they would have captured or killed all their enemies.
Chronicles

1 What did Douglas ask his knights to do?
2 What did they succeed in doing?
3 According to Froissart, what would have happened, if the Scots had had more men?

Among the prisoners taken by the Scots were Sir Henry and Sir Ralph Percy.

C Why did the Scots win the Battle of Otterburn?

It is difficult to understand why the Scots won at Otterburn. Froissart says that the English outnumbered them by nearly three to one. Froissart often makes mistakes when he gives the sizes of armies. It is quite likely he was wrong this time, as well. Even so, there would still be a problem. In nearly every other battle between the English and the Scots, the English won. Froissart himself seems puzzled. He says of Otterburn:

Document One
Though the English outnumbered the Scots, and were brave and skilful soldiers, and though at first they drove back the Scots, yet in the end, the Scots won the battle.
Chronicles

Here is the only explanation Froissart can find:

Document Two
The English were much more tired than the Scots, for they had come that same day from Newcastle. Also, they went at a great pace, which meant they arrived out of breath. As for the Scots, they were fresh, and had rested well.
Chronicles

1 According to Froissart, why were the English unable to fight as well as the Scots?

An English monk says this about Otterburn:

Document Three
The defeat at Otterburn was due in the first place to the reckless behaviour of Sir Henry Percy. He led our troops to battle in such a hurry that they were in disorder. The second reason was that the English were confused by the darkness. They could not tell the Scots from their own men, since they all spoke the same language. As a result, the English often killed each other. The third reason was that the Bishop of Durham did not bring help, as he had promised. He was close at hand with a large force. But because night was falling, he refused to go any further. Instead, he went to Newcastle. If he had waited until sunrise to enter the town, the women would have pelted him with stones, in revenge for their husbands who died in the battle.
The Westminster Chronicle

1 What is the first reason the monk gives for the defeat of the English?
2 Do you think Froissart would have agreed with this? (Look at Document Two of this section, and Document One of the last section.)
3 What is the second reason the monk gives for the defeat of the English?
4 Do you agree with this? (Was it any easier for the Scots to fight in the dark, do you suppose?)
5 What is the third reason the monk gives for the defeat of the English?
6 Would Froissart have agreed with this, do you suppose? (Look back to Document One in the last section. There, Froissart says why, in his opinion, the Bishop was not at the battle.)

Though he does not give it as a reason, we also have a clue from Froissart. He says of the battle:

Document Four
Knights and squires were so close together, fighting had to hand, that neither side was able to use its archers.
Chronicles

1 According to Froissart, which weapon was not used at Otterburn? Why?

Froissart only mentions in passing that the English could not use their archers. But the fact that they were unable to do so was, perhaps, the main reason for their defeat. If you look at Document One, page 8 you will see what happened when a Scottish army had to fight English archers.

OLIVER
FREY

D Sir Matthew Redmayne and Sir James Lindsay

Sir Matthew Redmayne was an Englishman, and Sir James Lindsay was a Scot. They both fought at the Battle of Otterburn. The monk who wrote the Westminster Chronicle says that while Sir Henry Percy attacked the Scots from the front, Sir Matthew Redmayne attacked them from the rear. He describes how Sir Henry Percy was defeated and goes on:

Document One
But on the other side, Sir Matthew Redmayne fought a very different battle. He made such a strong attack that the Scots who were against him turned tail and fled. He gave orders that every one of them should be killed, except those who could pay 100 marks for a ransom. Before returning home in triumph, he carried the chase to the Scottish border, dealing death and mortal wounds all the way. Among his prisoners was Sir James Lindsay.
The Westminster Chronicle.

According to the monk of Westminster:

1 What did the Scots do, when Sir Matthew Redmayne attacked them?
2 How far did Redmayne chase the Scots?
3 Who was one of Redmayne's prisoners?

Froissart tells a very different story:

Document Two
Sir Matthew Redmayne saw his men flee and so he took his horse, and left to save himself. Sir James Lindsay went after him. He came so close to him that he might have struck him with his spear. Instead, he said, 'Turn Sir Knight. It is shameful to run away like this.'

Sir Matthew said nothing, but spurred his horse even more. The chase went on for three miles, but in the end, Sir Matthew's horse tripped and fell under him. He drew his sword to defend himself. The Scot tried to strike him with his spear, but Sir Matthew dodged the blow, and the spear struck in the ground. Sir Matthew cut it in two with his sword. Then Sir James got off his horse, and took a little battle axe. With it he attacked Sir Matthew. They fought together for a long time, but in the end, Sir Matthew was so out of breath that he had to surrender.

'Well, sir,' he said, 'I am your prisoner, but I would like to go to Newcastle. If you will allow me, I will promise to come to Scotland in fifteen days to pay my ransom.' 'I agree,' said Lindsay. Then each man took his horse, and they said farewell to each other.
Chronicles

1 Why did Sir Matthew leave the battle?
2 Who rode after him?
3 Describe the fight between the two men.
4 Why did Sir Matthew have to surrender?
5 What promise did he make?

Figure 1 The Bishop of Durham captures Sir James Lindsay

Here is what happened to Sir James Lindsay:

Document Three
Sir James Lindsay could not find the way. It was dark, and there was a mist. Before he had ridden a mile, he met the Bishop of Durham, who had more than 500 Englishmen with him. He might have escaped, but he thought they were Scots. When he was among them, one of them asked him who he was. 'I am Sir James Lindsay,' he said. When the Bishop heard these words he said, 'Lindsay, you are my prisoner. You must come with me to Newcastle.'
Chronicles

1 How was Sir James Lindsay captured?
2 Where was he taken?

At Newcastle, Lindsay and Redmayne met. This is what they said to each other:

Document Four
'Well, Sir James,' said Sir Matthew, 'what brings you here?'
'Ill fortune brings me here,' said Sir James. 'As soon as I left you, I met the Bishop of Durham and I am now his prisoner. I do not think you will have to come to Scotland to pay your ransom. I think instead, we should exchange each other, if the Bishop will allow it.' 'I am sure we shall agree right well,' said Sir Matthew. 'Today you shall have dinner with me.' And the two knights dined together in Newcastle.
Chronicles

1 What agreement did the two knights make?

We have, then, two stories, one told by the monk of Westminster, and one by Froissart. There is no way of knowing which is right. Do they agree on anything at all? If so, that is probably as close as we shall come to the truth.

5 Henry V and the Battle of Agincourt

A Introduction

When Edward III died in 1377, his grandson, Richard II, became King. Richard was only ten years old. During the first part of his reign there were a few chevauchées through France. But when the King came of age he showed no interest in fighting the French. Instead, he tried to make peace. In 1396, he married a French princess.

In 1399, Richard was deposed by Henry Bolingbroke who had himself crowned as Henry IV. Henry was warlike enough, but he had troubles at home. Powerful nobles rebelled against him, while Owen Glendower led a revolt of the Welsh that lasted for years. Henry IV died in 1413. It was left to his son, Henry V, to lead the first serious invasion of France that there had been for a long time. You are going to read about it in this chapter.

It is August 1415. We are in Southampton. Out in the Solent are hundreds of ships, while the town itself is full of soldiers. We will stop and talk to one of them.

'What is happening here?'

'Our King is gathering an army to invade France.'

'Why is he doing that?'

'He is the rightful King of France. He is going to claim his throne. But there is another reason, I think.'

'Please tell us what it is.'

'Our present King's father took the throne by force. Many a noble thought that if Henry could overthrow the rightful King, then there could be nothing wrong in overthrowing Henry. He had to fight hard to keep his throne. Even our new King has had the same problem. Sir John Oldcastle led a rebellion against him. Just a few days ago he had to execute the Earl of Cambridge, Lord Scrope and Sir Thomas Grey for conspiring against him.'

'What has that to do with invading France?'

'Don't you see that if the King leads his nobles against the French, they will unite behind him? There is nothing like success in war to draw men together. The King is taking with him the sons of several men executed by his father. If, together, they can win a great victory over the French, all their quarrels will be forgotten.'

'But what if the French win?'

'The French will not win.'

'How can you be sure?'

'For one thing, the King of France, Charles VI, is insane much of the time. One day he was out riding, when, suddenly, he ran wild. He killed several of his courtiers before he was overpowered. Since then he has often had bouts of madness. Sometimes he imagines he is made of glass, and is frightened that someone will break him.'

'Surely there are plenty of great nobles who could rule France while the King is ill?'

'There are indeed. But they are busy quarrelling with each other. John the Fearless, Duke of Burgundy, and Louis, Duke of Orleans were deadly rivals. Louis took as his badge a cudgel, showing he meant to beat down his enemies. John then took as his badge a carpenter's plane. That showed what he meant to do to the cudgel. One dark night in 1407, John of Burgundy had Louis of Orleans murdered. His assassins scattered his brains all over the road. They also cut off his right hand to stop it raising the devil. Since then, the French nobles have been divided. Some support the Duke of Burgundy. Others are the men who had been loyal to the Duke

Figure 1 Henry V hears of the Earl of Cambridge's plot to assassinate him

Figure 2 King Henry V

of Orleans. Their leader is the Count of Armagnac.

'At present, it is the Armagnacs who rule France in the King's name. But I do not think they will attack us. If they did, they would be looking over their shoulders the whole time, through fear of the Burgundians.'

'Are you pleased you are going to France?'

'Yes, of course. I am looking forward to some excitement. Also, with luck, I shall capture some wealthy Frenchmen. I will hold them to ransom and make my fortune.'

The English fleet set sail on August 11th 1415. As it made its way along the coast of the Isle of Wight, there were swans swimming among the ships. The men saw that as a happy omen.

1 How did Richard II feel about fighting the French?
2 Why was Henry IV unable to attack France?
3 Henry V was expecting trouble from his nobles. How would invading France help him solve that problem?
4 What was the matter with Charles VI of France?
5 Who murdered the Duke of Orleans?
6 What are the two rival groups of nobles in France?
7 Which group is governing France?
8 Why will they be unwilling to attack the English?
9 Why is the soldier pleased he is going to France?

B The Siege of Harfleur

The English landed near Harfleur on August 14th 1415. The town was not large, but it had strong defences. There were high walls, with towers. There were deep ditches, the one on the west side being filled with water. Also, outside each of the three gates there was a barbican. Figure 1 will show you what this was. The barbican on the west side of the town was particularly strong.

This is how the English besieged Harfleur:

Document One

The King stayed up night and day, placing his siege engines and guns close to the town. He set up screens in front of his artillery to protect it from the shots of the enemy. These were made of long, thick planks. When the top was pulled down, the bottom was lifted up to give a view of the town. The guns then fired their stones.

The King had trenches dug between the guns and the town. These trenches protected the men who served the guns, in case of enemy sallies. Those who were on guard duty dug without stopping, day after day. All the time, they gained ground towards the barbican. They did not cease until they could see the water in the ditch.

Meanwhile, from every side, our King pounded the barbican and walls with his guns and siege engines. Within a few days, much of the barbican had been demolished. Also, the walls and towers were made defenceless, because their ramparts had been destroyed. At the same time, almost as far as the middle of the town, buildings were destroyed, or so badly damaged that they threatened to fall.

Gesta Henrici Quinti

Notes: 'sally' – garrison coming out of fortress to attack besiegers
'ramparts' – tops of walls, where defenders stood

1 Look at Figure 2. Find a screen like the ones described in the first paragraph of this document. Explain, in your own words, how it worked. (Here, it is protecting archers, and not guns.)

Figure 1 Barbican. This one is at York.

2 Why did the King have trenches dug in front of the guns?

3 What other trenches were dug? (See Figure 3.)

4 What happened to the barbican, the walls and towers, and the town?

This is how the French defended themselves:

Document Two

Cleverly using their guns, catapults and engines, they did what damage they could from the barbican and from the walls and towers, as long as they could be defended. Afterwards, they fought from inside the ruins, from behind

Figure 2 Besieging a town

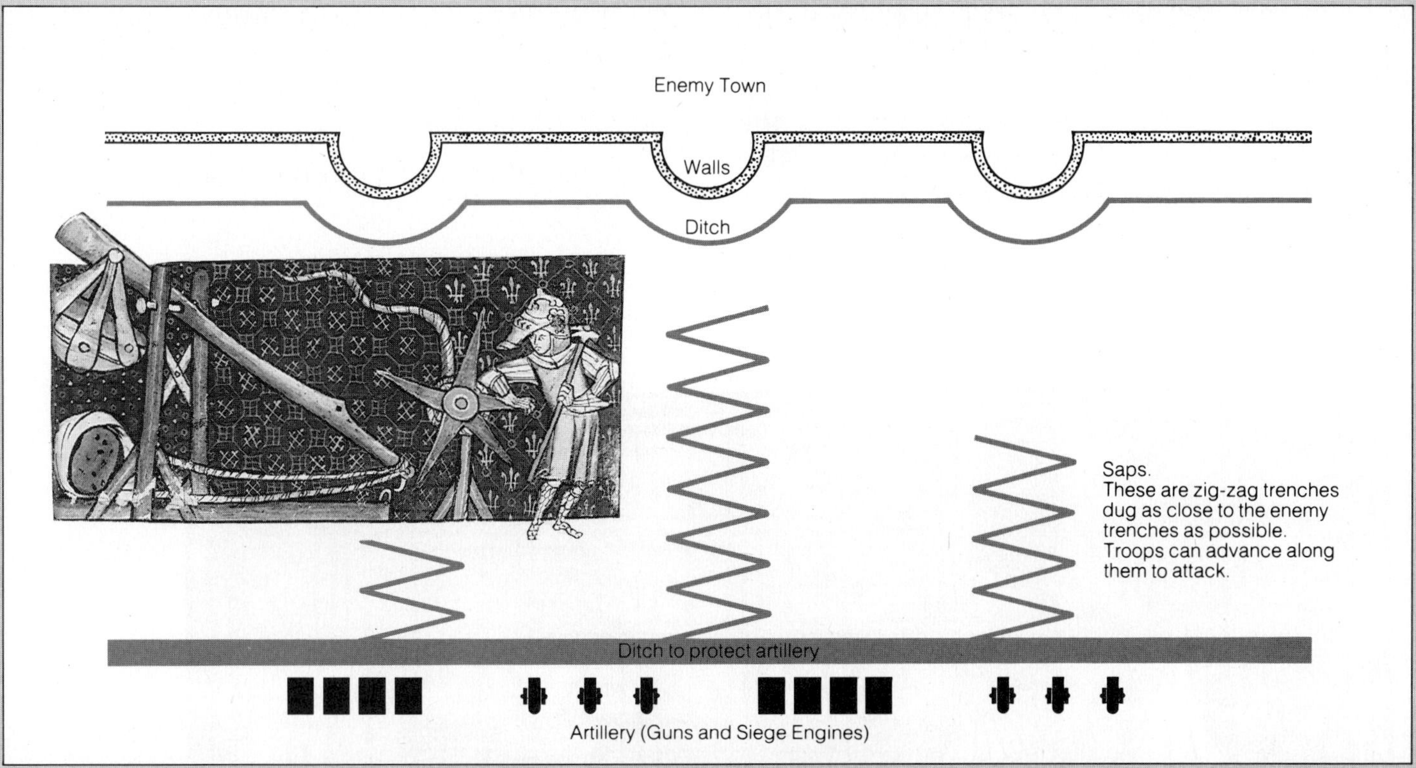

Figure 3 Siege works

screens, and through shattered openings in the walls. And, however much our guns damaged the defences by day, by night the enemy made them good. On top of the walls they placed timber and tubs filled with earth, sand, dung or stones. Inside the walls that were falling down, they piled bundles of faggots, packed with earth, clay and dung. They also covered the streets of the town quite thickly with earth, clay and dung, to swallow up the stones from our guns, when they landed. This was to stop them bursting into splinters and hurting any of the besieged.

Also, the enemy had made ready on the walls, jars filled with burning powders, sulphur and quicklime, to throw in the eyes of our men, if they should attack. There were also barrels of oil and burning fat, to set fire to our siege equipment, when brought up to attack. Indeed, no people under siege could have resisted better than they did.

Gesta Henrici Quinti

1 What weapons did the defenders fire?
2 Where did they fight, after the walls had been damaged?
3 How did they repair the walls?
4 What did they spread on the streets of the town? Why?
5 What did they have ready to throw?

Here are some successes the defenders had:

Document Three

a The King decided to attack by means of mines, that is to undermine the walls with passages below the ground. But this was begun in full view of the enemy, because it could not be done in any other place. As a result, it was defeated by the enemy who used counter-mines.

b. The King ordered bundles of faggots ten feet long, to fill up the ditches. He also had wooden towers prepared, as high as the walls. But he discovered that the enemy had materials to set fire to the faggots, while our men were in the ditch. That made him abandon his plan.

c. Our enemies who were in the strongest barbican made a sally against our guard facing

them. Because our men were lazy, and not paying attention, the French set fire to their defences. At last, by God's will, the fire was put out and the enemy driven away. But the enemy mocked us for being only half awake, and not keeping a better watch.
Gesta Henrici Quinti

1 Why were the English mines a failure?
2 What did the King plan to use, to fill the ditches? Why did he give up the idea?
3 Which Frenchmen made a sally?
4 What did they succeed in doing?

Figure 4 Citizens surrender a town

5 According to the Chronicle, why were the French driven back?
6 Why did the French laugh at the English?

The day after the French made their sally from the barbican, this happened:

Document Four
On the morrow, God remembered us, and gave us a victory over that barbican, which the French had said could never be taken.

During the night, the ditch was filled with long bundles of faggots. In the morning, fire was shot into the barbican by arrows. Then our men crossed the ditch, and took the stronger part of the barbican. They attacked those of the French who offered to fight, and who were doing their best to put out the flames. At last, the French fled, because of our attack, and because of the fire. They ran inside the walls, blocking the entrance as well as they could, with timber, earth, stone and dung.

Our men tried to put out the blaze, but the fire burnt for another two or three days. Indeed, the smoke from the dung could not be smothered for a fortnight.
Gesta Henrici Quinti

Note: The ditch was full of water at this point, so there was no danger of the French setting the faggots on fire.

1 How was the barbican set on fire?
2 How did the English cross the ditch?
3 Why did the French run away?
4 Where did they go? How did they prevent the English from following them?

Even though they had lost the strongest part of their defences, the French still refused to surrender. This is what happened next:

Document Five
The King ordered his army to be ready to storm the walls the following day. Towards evening he began to batter the enemy more than usual, with his cannon. This was to prevent them from sleeping, and so make them easier to defeat on the morrow.

Figure 5 Stone cannon balls, Museum of Artillery, Woolwich. The ruler, in front of the cannon balls is 30 centimetres long. Measure a football, to see how it compares.
If one of these balls hit a hard surface, it would burst into pieces which would fly everywhere. Read *Document Two* to see how the people of Harfleur stopped this happening.

But God was merciful to His people, and spared them the bloodshed that there would have been in storming the town. Instead, He struck terror into our enemies. They had lost heart when the barbican fell; they were frightened that the town would be sacked; they were troubled by our hail of stones; they had almost given up hope of a rescue by the French army. As a result, they told our King that they would surrender the town, unless the French army came and relieved it before one o'clock in the afternoon of the next Sunday.

Our King accepted these terms, and there was no more fighting.
Gesta Henrici Quinti

1 What did the King decide to do on the following day?
2 What did he do in the meantime?
3 Give some of the reasons why the people of Harfleur had lost heart.
4 On what condition did the town agree to surrender?

By the following Sunday there was still no sign of the French army, so Harfleur surrendered. The siege had lasted five weeks. Henry accepted the keys of the town from its governor, and treated him and many of the leading citizens to a banquet. The next day he entered the town. The rich people were made prisoners and held to ransom. The poor people were driven from their homes, to make room for settlers from England.

C The March to Calais

The King decides on the March

After taking Harfleur, King Henry V challenged the Dauphin to a duel. The Dauphin was the eldest son of the French King, Charles VI. Here is the challenge:

Document One

I have many times, and in many ways sought peace, but I have been unable to find it. War means the deaths of men, the destruction of countries, the sorrow of women and children. It means so many evils that all good Christians must regret it. I am looking for every possible way to avoid these evils. Therefore I offer to place our quarrel at the will of God, in a duel between My Person and Yours. If God gives me the victory, then the crown of France shall be given to me on the death of the King, your father.

Thomas Rymer, *Foedera*

1 What does Henry say he is looking for? Do you think this is true?

Figure 1 The March to Calais

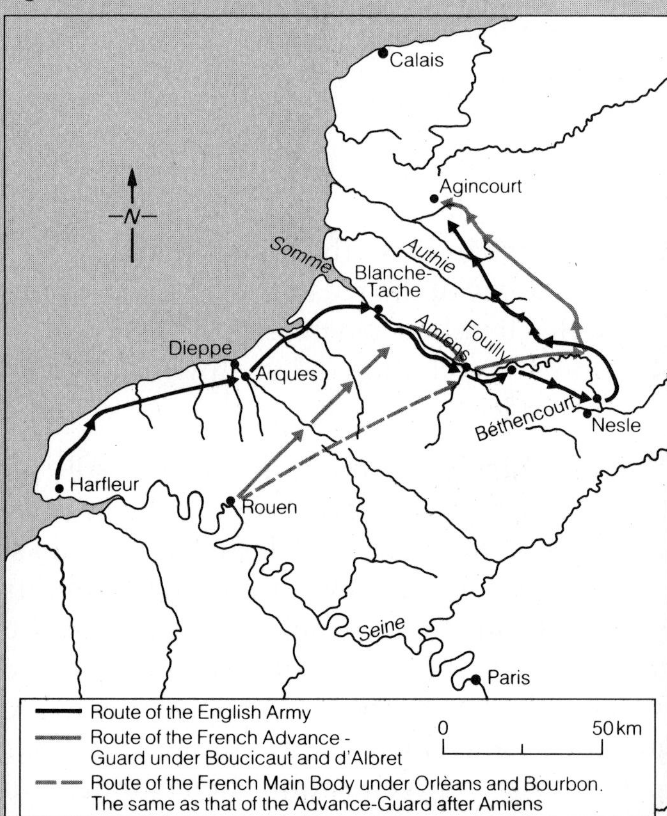

2 What are some of the evils of war that he mentions?

3 What does he want to do about them?

4 What does Henry mean when he says the duel will 'place our quarrel at the will of God'?

5 What will Henry have, if he wins the duel?

Henry was a strong man, aged 28. The Dauphin was a sickly youth of 19, and he ignored Henry's challenge. Henry wondered what to do next. He could have taken his army straight back to England, but so far he had only captured one French town. That did not seem very much. Henry felt he must do something more, if his invasion of France was to be a success. He decided that the best idea would be to make a chevauchée through Normandy. He would march to Calais, which was in English hands, and go home from there.

If you do not know what a chevauchée was, then you should read Chapter Two, Section E.

There was one thing wrong with Henry's plan. He had already lost much of his army. Some men had been killed in the siege of Harfleur. After the town had fallen he had given it a garrison of 1200 soldiers. Some men had deserted. Most important of all, many had died of disease, and even more had been sent home because they were sick. As far as we can tell, Henry had brought 9000 men to France. He now had only 6000 to make his chevauchée. Many of the English nobles were against the chevauchée, but Henry was determined to have his way. This is what he told his Council:

Document Two

Even if our enemies have the greatest of armies, I will trust in God. They shall hurt neither my army nor me. If I went home now, they would say that through fear I had run away. But I have a mind, my brave men, to meet all dangers, rather than let them mock your King. With the help of God, we shall go

Figure 2 Soldiers on the march

unhurt; if they try to stop us, we shall win a great and glorious victory.
Tito Livio, *Vita Henrici Quinti*

According to Henry:
1 Who will protect him and his army?
2 What would the French think, if the English went straight home?
3 What will happen if the French try to stop the English?

How the English behaved on the March

The English began their march on October 9th. This is what happened two days later:

Document Three
Pressing forward on the march, we arrived before the town of Arques. Here there was a castle guarding a narrow bridge. The garrison shot stones at us to prevent us from coming close. The stones, however, by God's will, did not hurt anyone.

After a short time, the king sent to the garrison to ask them to let us pass. After some argument, they allowed the King to pass. They also gave him bread and wine for his army. They did this in order to save their town and the villages around from being burnt.
Gesta Henrici Quinti

1 What did the garrison of Arques do, when the English first arrived?
2 Why, in the end, did they agree to help the English?

Others towns paid ransom, like Arques, but not all. When the English arrived at Nesle, the citizens covered their walls with red cloths. That showed they were going to defy the English. Here is what happened:

Document Four
We were lodged in little villages near the walled town of Nesle. The King sent word to the townspeople to ransom the villages from burning. But when they refused, he ordered the villages to be set on fire, and completely destroyed.
Gesta Henrici Quinti

1 What did the King order the people of Nesle to do?
2 What happened when they refused?
3 No damage was done to Nesle itself. Why was that, do you suppose?

King Henry made some strict rules for his troops. Here is one on them:

Document Five

No man shall rob or pillage a church of any goods or ornaments that belong to it. Nor shall he slay any monk or priest, unless he is armed, on pain of death. No man shall kill or rape any woman, on pain of death. No man shall take prisoner any monk or priest, unless he is armed, or any woman, on pain of imprisonment.

Statutes to be kept in time of war

1 Which buildings does this rule protect?
2 Which people does it protect?

Here is what happened to a soldier who disobeyed the King:

Document Six

There was brought to the King a certain robber, an Englishman. In spite of the laws of God and the King, he had stolen from a church a pyx. That pyx was found in his sleeve. After sentence had been passed he was hanged. Thus the King punished the man for the crime that he had done against God.

Gesta Henrici Quinti

Figure 3 Army transport

Note: 'pyx' – small box for the bread used in the service of the Mass

1 According to the writer, whose laws had the man broken?
2 How was he punished?

Henry allowed his soldiers to kill any ordinary Frenchmen they might find. As you have seen, he himself ordered villages to be destroyed. But he ordered his men to spare church buildings, monks, priests and women. If you look again at Document Two, you will understand the reason for this. According to Henry, whose help did he need, if he was to reach Calais in safety?

Events on the March

On their way to Calais the English had to cross a number of rivers. The largest of these was the River Somme. Henry hoped to cross it at the ford of Blanche-Tache. It was the same ford that Edward III had used in the Crécy campaign of 1346. But Henry was dismayed to hear that it was guarded by a large French army. All he could do was to march east, and hope to find another place to cross. What had the French done to the bridges, do you suppose?

The English had brought enough supplies for eight days, and these were running short. This is what the men were thinking:

Document Seven

We thought only of this: our food would soon run out. Meanwhile, the enemy was going ahead of us, and laying waste the countryside. By the time we reached the head of the river we would be starving. Then the great army of the French would destroy us, for we were very few, and we would be weak from lack of food.

Many of the army looked up in bitterness to Heaven, and called on the Virgin and Saint George. They begged them to ask God to spare us, who sought not war but peace, and bring us in triumph to Calais.

Gesta Henrici Quinti

1 How did the French stop the English from finding food?
2 What would be the plight of the English, by the time they reached the head of the river?
3 What would happen to them, then?
4 To whom did many of the army pray? What did they ask?

After the English had marched nearly 70 miles up the Somme, they had good news:

Document Eight

And suddenly, by God's will, news was brought to the King that three miles away there was a ford across the Somme. And when the River Somme was reached, there were found two places where it could be crossed. The water reached only a little higher than a horse's belly. The approach to these two places was by two long, narrow causeways, which ran over a marsh. These, the French had broken in the middle, so that it was only possible to ride across the broken parts in single file.

First, the King sent across a number of men-at-arms and archers, to protect the rest of the army when climbing the bank. He then ordered the broken parts to be filled in with wood, bundles of faggots and straw, until it was possible for three men to ride abreast.

He ordered that the baggage of the army should cross by one of the causeways, and the fighting men at the other. He himself stood at the entrance of the latter. This was to prevent the throng of men becoming tightly packed, and choking the narrow passage. Using these two places, the strength of the army greatly increased on the other side of the water.

Gesta Henrici Quinti

1 At how many places was it possible to cross the Somme?
2 What had the French done, to make it difficult to reach the fords?
3 Pretend you are Henry V. Write your orders for the crossing of the Somme.

This is what happened while the main body of the English army was crossing the river:

Document Nine

Before a hundred of our men had waded across the river, enemy cavalry appeared. They sent their swifter riders on ahead, to find out whether it was possible to drive us back.

Our mounted patrols went out to meet them, and they were slow in bringing up their forces. Meanwhile, many more of our men had crossed the river. The French did not dare to attack us, and vanished from our sight.

Gesta Henrici Quinti

1 Who appeared, after a few of the English had crossed the river?
2 Why did they not attack the English?

You will probably wonder why there were not enough of the French to stop the English crossing the Somme. You will find the answer, if you look at the map on page 50. The English had left the river at Fouilly, and marched straight to Béthencourt. That meant they cut off a big bend in the river. The French who were on the north side of the river could not keep up with them.

Once they had crossed the Somme, the English were hopeful:

Document Ten
We spent a cheerful night. We were very pleased that we had shortened our march. Also, we hoped that the enemy army which was waiting for us would be unwilling to follow us to do battle.
Gesta Henrici Quinti

Figure 4 The English cross the River Somme

1 Why were the English pleased?
2 What did they hope the French army would be unwilling to do?

Soon, however, the English saw something that alarmed them:

Document Eleven
After we had gone past the town of Péronne, we found the roads badly churned up by the French army. They looked as if they had been crossed by many thousands of men. We feared there would soon be a battle, and we raised our hearts and eyes to Heaven. We called out, asking God to have pity on us, and in His goodness, save us from the violence of the French.
Gesta Henrici Quinti

1 What had happened to the roads near Péronne?
2 What did this seem to prove?
3 What were the English soldiers afraid of?

This what happened three days later:

Document Twelve
We were moving down a valley towards a river when word was brought to our King that an enemy force of many thousands was on the other side.

We crossed over the river as quickly as possible. But, just as we reached the top of the hill, we saw the grim-looking ranks of the French. They were in compact masses, their numbers being very much greater than our own. At length, they took up a position facing us. They filled a huge field like a swarm of locusts, and there was only a small valley between us and them.
Gesta Henrici Quinti

1 What news was brought to the King?
2 What did the English see, when they reached the top of the hill?

D The Battle of Agincourt

Before the Battle

It was already late when the English and French armies met. There was no battle that day. Here is what happened during the night:

Document One

We could hear the enemy calling out, some wanting their servants, and some their friends. Our men had begun to do the same, but the King ordered silence. Any gentleman who disobeyed the royal order was to lose his horse and armour. Any common soldier who did so was to lose his right ear.

Our enemies noted how still and silent we were. They thought that we were afraid, and were trying to escape during the night. They lit fires, and kept watch on the fields and roads. They were so sure of defeating us that they cast dice for our King and his nobles.

Gesta Henrici Quinti

Figure 1 The Battle of Agincourt

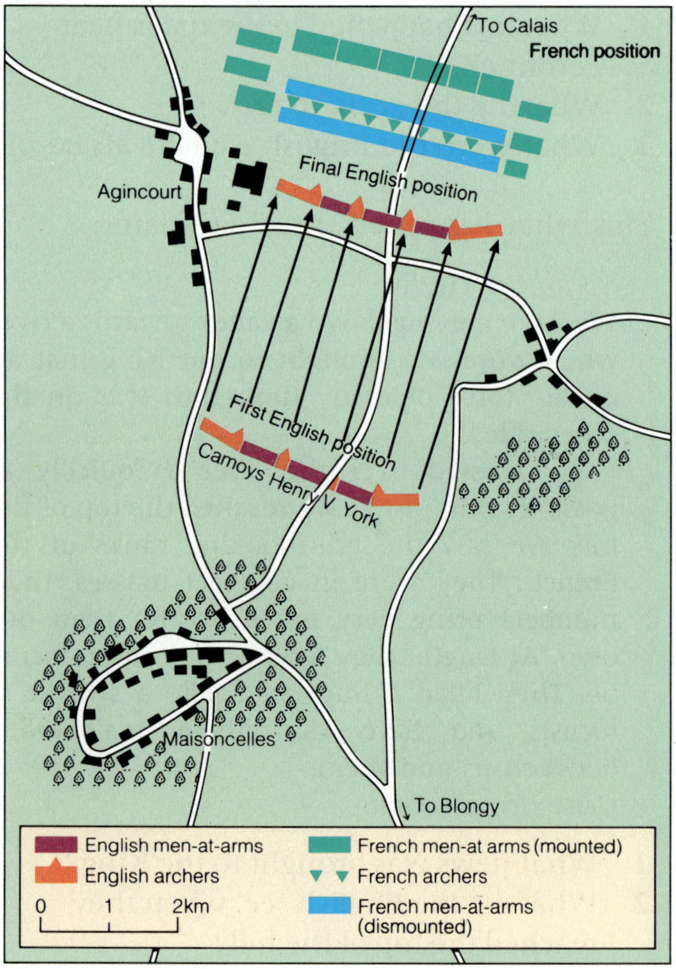

1 What did the English hear from the French camp?
2 Why did Henry order his men to keep quiet, do you suppose? (Remember, they were going to fight a battle the next day.)
3 What were the punishments for disobeying this order?
4 What did the French think the English were trying to do?
5 What shows that the French were sure they would win?

In the morning, the French drew up their army for battle:

Document Two

They arrayed themselves in battle lines in that field called the field of Agincourt. The number of them was terrifying. They placed squadrons of cavalry, many hundreds strong, on each flank of their vanguard. And that vanguard

Figure 2 Knights arming for battle

Figure 3 The Battle of Agincourt. This picture is full of mistakes. When you have read the documents, see how many you can find.

was drawn from all their nobles and the pick of their forces. With its forest of spears, and the great number of helmets gleaming, it was, I would guess, thirty times more than all our men put together.

The men of their rearguard were all mounted, as if more ready to flee than to fight. Compared to our men, they were a multitude not to be counted.
Gesta Henrici Quinti

1 Study the battle plan (Figure 1), and find:
  a. The French vanguard.
  b. The cavalry on its flanks.
  c. The French rearguard.
2 According to the chronicle, how many times did the French vanguard outnumber the entire English army? (This is what it may have seemed to the writer, but the figure is far too high.)
3 According to the chronicle, why was the French rearguard mounted?
4 What was the real reason, do you suppose? (What would the rearguard have done, if the vanguard had put the English to flight?)

This is how Henry drew up the English army:

Document Three
Our King, after offering praises to God, and hearing Mass, made ready for the field. As he had so few men, he drew up only a single line of battle. Between each body of men-at-arms, he placed wedges of his archers. He had them drive pointed stakes in front of them, in case of a cavalry charge. Meanwhile the enemy, for some reason known to God but not to me, kept his distance.
Gesta Henrici Quinti

1 Study the battle plan and find:
   a. The English men-at-arms.
   b. The English archers.
2 Look at the battle plan of Crécy on page 15. How is the English line of battle the same? How is it different?
3 What did the archers do, to protect themselves from cavalry?
4 What did the French do, while the English were drawing up their line of battle?

Figure 4 Brass of Thomas, Lord Comoys and his wife. Lord Comoys commanded the left of the English battle line at Agincourt.

The Battle

As you have seen, the French were in no hurry to attack:

Document Four
Most of the day, the two armies stood still, neither moving a foot towards the other. The King realised our enemies were putting off their attack, and simply blocking our road to Calais. He thought they might be waiting for reinforcements. It was also possible that they knew how short we were of food. They might have thought they could overcome us with hunger, not daring to do so by the sword. And so he decided to advance towards them. At the same time the enemy, too, advanced towards us.
Gesta Henrici Quinti

1 What did both armies do, for most of the day?
2 Why might the French have been waiting?
3 What did Henry do, in the end?

This is how the fighting began:

Document Five
The French cavalry who were on their flanks made charges against the archers who were on our flanks. But soon, by God's will, they were forced to fall back under showers of arrows. Many were stopped by the stakes that were driven into the ground. Many were killed before they had fled very far, by the stinging hail of missiles.
Gesta Henrici Quinti

1 Which men in the French army were the first to attack?
2 Why did their attack fail?
3 What happened to many of them, as they fled?

Now the French vanguard attacked. You will remember that it was made up of dismounted men-at-arms:

Document Six
The French vanguard divided into three columns, and attacked our line of battle where

our men-at-arms were. They hurled themselves against our men in such a fierce charge that they forced them back almost a spear's length.

And then the battle raged at its fiercest. Our archers loosed their sharp-pointed arrows into the enemy's flanks, keeping up the fight without pause. When their arrows were all used up, they seized axes, stakes, swords and spearheads that were lying about. With these, they struck down, hacked and stabbed the enemy. For Almighty God increased the strength of our men, which dire want of food had weakened. He also took away their fear and gave them brave hearts.

Moreover, God turned His face away from our enemies. He broke their strength – the bow, the shield, the sword and the line of battle. Never before had so many fine warriors been so confused, faint-hearted and unmanly.
Gesta Henrici Quinti

Figure 5 Henry V on his charger

1 Where did the French vanguard attack the English battle line?
2 What did the French succeed in doing, at first?
3 Why were the French men-at-arms unable to follow up their attack, do you think? (The chronicle gives you a good clue.)
4 According to the chronicle how did God help the English? What did He do to the French?

This was how the battle continued:

Document Seven
Some of the French, killed at the start of the battle, fell at the front. So great was the violence and pressure of the mass of men behind, that the living fell on top of the dead. Others, falling on top of the living, were killed as well. The result was a great heap of the slain and of those lying crushed in between. Our men climbed up these heaps, which had risen above a man's height, and killed their enemies down below with swords, axes and other weapons.

At last, after two or three hours, the French vanguard was broken. Our men then began to pull the heaps apart. They separated the living from the dead, meaning to hold them to ransom.
Gesta Henrici Quinti

1 Explain how there came to be heaps of Frenchmen, in front of the English line.
2 What does this tell you about the discipline in the French army?
3 Why did the English want to rescue the Frenchmen who were still alive?

Meanwhile, several hundred French peasants were looting the English baggage. It seemed likely that the English army might be attacked from the rear. There was another danger, as well:

Document Eight
A shout went up that the enemy's mounted rearguard was about to make an attack on us. We were few and weary; they were a great many, and still fresh. Immediately, the prisoners were killed, either by their captors, or by others. This was to prevent them turning on us in the fighting that was about to happen.

But the enemy soldiers soon had the bitter taste of our arrows, and our army marched towards them. After a short time they fled, leaving their baggage waggons behind. These were filled with food and weapons.
Gesta Henrici Quinti

1 Which part of the French army was preparing to attack?
2 Why was the attack likely to be dangerous?
3 What did the English do with their prisoners? Why?
4 Why did the French run away?
5 What did they leave behind?

The prisoners were killed on orders from the King. Some were burnt to death in a hut where they had been locked. Henry had to send 200 archers to do the killing, because most of his men who had prisoners wanted to keep them. Why was that, do you think? In fact, not all the prisoners were killed. One that survived was the Duke of Orleans. He was to spend 25 years in England, before he was allowed to return to France. (See Figure 1, page 10.)

After the Battle

The chronicle describes the battle field, after the fighting:

Document Nine
When the battle had ended, we who had gained the victory came back through the

Figure 6 After the battle. The French prisoners and dead are stripped of their armour.

masses and mounds and heaps of the slain. We saw them with sorrow and tears. It made us sad to think that so many famous warriors had died at our hands, who had no wish to kill them. And if that sight made us take pity, how much more must it have grieved their own people. And I truly believe that any man with a heart of flesh, or even of stone, would have been reduced to tears had he seen the horrible deaths and dreadful wounds of so many Christian men.

They had been plundered, and they were all as naked as the day they were born.

Gesta Henrici Quinti

1 How did the author of the chronicle feel, when he saw the French dead? Explain in your own words.

The chronicle says this about the numbers killed on both sides:

Document Ten

The French say that there were more than 60 000 in their army. Our little band was 6 000 fighting men. Of the great French host there fell three dukes, five counts, more than ninety barons, some 1 500 knights, and between four and five thousand other gentlemen.

There was great rejoicing among our folk and also great amazement. Out of our little band there were slain no more than nine or ten persons.

But far be it from our people to say that the victory was due to their own glory or strength. It was due to God alone, from Whom is every victory.

Gesta Henrici Quinti

According to the chronicle:

1 How many times did the French outnumber the English?
2 How many French nobles were killed?
3 Roughly, how many knights and gentlemen were killed?
4 Is there any figure for ordinary French soldiers killed?
5 How many English were killed?
6 Who was responsible for the victory?

Figure 7 Battlefield of Agincourt. Most of the fighting was to the left of the road which is in the middle of the picture.

Different chronicles give different figures for the numbers killed. For example, the French said that 600 English were killed. We shall never know the truth. All we can say for certain is that the French lost far more than the English.

Laden with plunder, the English army marched slowly to Calais. From there it sailed to England. This is how the English felt about their King:

Document Eleven

Our older men do not remember any prince having commanded his soldiers on the march with more effort, bravery or kindness. Nor do they remember any who fought more bravely in battle. Nor was there any king of England who achieved so much in so short a time, and returned home with so great and glorious a triumph. To God alone be the honour and the glory, for ever and ever. Amen.

Gesta Henrici Quinti

1 Imagine you are a Frenchman. Say what you think of Henry V.

E The Siege of Rouen

In 1417, Henry V invaded France for a second time. Before he did so, he made an alliance with John the Fearless of Burgundy. Many French soldiers went to fight the Burgundians, so Henry was able to conquer Normandy. The most important event was the siege of the capital of Normandy, Rouen.

The siege began in July 1418. Henry's army surrounded the town with a ditch. They also built wooden towers in which they mounted guns. By October, the people of Rouen were running short of food. An Englishman who was at the siege wrote a poem about their sufferings. Do not worry if you cannot quite understand all he says:

Document One

Meat and drink and other victual
In that city began to fail.
Save clean water and plenty too,
And vinegar to put thereto.
Their flesh save horsemeat had they none.
They ate up dogs, they ate up cats;
They ate up mice, horses and rats.
For a horses quarter, lean or fat,
One hundred shillings it was at.
A horse's head for half a pound,
A dog for the same money round.
For thirty pennies went a rat.
For two nobles went a cat.
For sixpence went a mouse,
They left but few in any house.
Onions and leeks, as will appear,
Were to them a food full dear.
Thereof was a piece a shilling.
He did well who got a pilling.
Then to die they did begin,
All that rich city within.
They died so fast on every day,
That men could not them in earth lay.
Even if a child should be dead,
The mother would not give it bread.
Nor would a child to its mother give;
Everyone tried himself to live,
As long as he could last.
Love and kindness both were past.

John Page, *The Siege of Rouen*

Notes: 'victual' – food
'pilling' – small piece

Figure 1 Siege. The attackers have built wooden towers and are using cannon, as the English did at Rouen.

1 What did the people of Rouen have to drink?
2 What did they have to eat?
3 What happened to the price of food?
4 How did the people of Rouen behave towards each other, when food became scarce?

To save food for themselves, the soldiers in Rouen drove 12,000 poor folk from the city. But the English would not let them pass. They had to stay in the ditch that surrounded the town. John Page describes their plight:

Document Two
There men might see a great pity,
A child of two years or of three
Go about to beg his bread,
For father and mother both were dead.
And under them the water stood,
And yet they lay crying after food.
Some had starved in that place to death,
And some had stopped both eyes and breath,
And some were crooked in the knees
And were now as lean as trees.
You saw a woman hold in her arm
Her own dead child, with nothing warm.
And babies sucking on the pap
Within a dead woman's lap.
There men might find it at last arrive
That twelve were dead to one alive.
And the dead knew nought of death
So secretly they gave up their breath.
Without a noise or any cry,
As if they slept, so did they die.
The Siege of Rouen

Note: Page says 'under them the water stood' because it had been raining hard.

A few of the people in the ditch lived, because the more kind-hearted of the English soldiers threw them food. On Christmas Day even King Henry sent them food. But he still refused to let them go. He told the defenders of Rouen that it was not he who had put the people in the ditch. Whom do you think was more to blame for this cruelty, the King, or the soldiers in Rouen?

By the beginning of January the town was completely out of food. The garrison agreed to surrender if no help arrived within nineteen days. No help came, so the town opened its gates to the English. Henry entered in triumph. The first thing he did was to attend a service of thanksgiving in the cathedral.

Figure 2 Siege

Figure 3 Town surrounded by an enemy camp

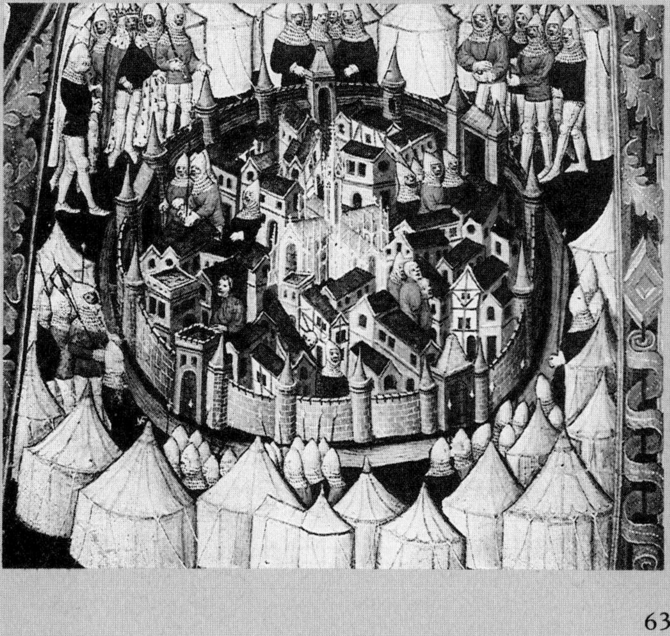

F Conclusion

While the English were overrunning Normandy, the Burgundians took much of France, including Paris. But John the Fearless decided that the English were becoming too powerful and must be stopped. He offered to meet the Armagnac leaders and make peace with them. This was agreed, and the Duke with a few of his followers came face to face with some of the Armagnacs. This was on a bridge at the town of Montereau. With the Armagnacs was the Dauphin Charles, then a boy of sixteen. Suddenly, one of the Armagnacs struck Duke John a violent blow. It broke his skull and killed him. People who were there said it was the Dauphin who gave the signal for the attack.

There was now no question of peace between the Burgundians and the Armagnacs.

Figure 1 France after the Treaty of Troyes, 1420

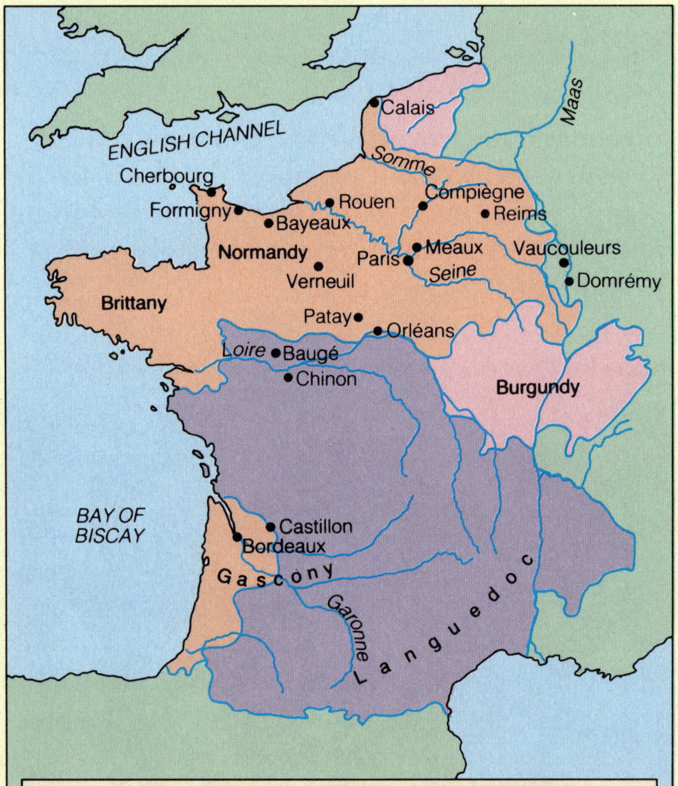

Instead, the new Duke of Burgundy, Philip the Good, made an alliance with the English. He promised King Henry that he would help him conquer the whole of France.

The following year, 1420, Charles VI of France was forced to sign the Treaty of Troyes. By this treaty he agreed that on his death, Henry V should become King of France. He also agreed that Henry should marry his daughter, Catherine. The wedding took place almost at once, and shortly afterwards Henry and Philip of Burgundy entered Paris in triumph. With them was poor, mad King Charles. A hundred years later, a monk showed the battered skull of John the Fearless to a French King. He remarked, 'Through this hole the English entered France.'

In 1421, Henry returned to England. He wanted to have his bride crowned as Queen and he wanted to raise money.

Meanwhile the Dauphin had not accepted the Treaty of Troyes. Obviously, he felt he should be King when his father died. Many Frenchmen supported him. It so happened that Henry's brother, the Duke of Clarence, heard that one of the Dauphin's armies was at Baugé, nearby. Clarence only had his men-at-arms with him, but he insisted on rushing to give battle. The Earl of Huntingdon advised him to wait for his archers. Clarence replied, 'If you are frightened, go home and look after the churchyard.' Clarence's men were heavily outnumbered, but he ordered them to attack none the less. They were defeated, and he was killed.

On hearing the news of the Battle of Baugé, Henry hurried back to France. The Dauphin and his followers had taken heart, they had control of much of France and they were prepared to fight. Henry began to storm towns and fortresses one by one, but it was a slow process. It must have seemed that the war would go on for ever. In his anger, Henry was very cruel to the men he captured. For example, he hanged the entire garrison of the

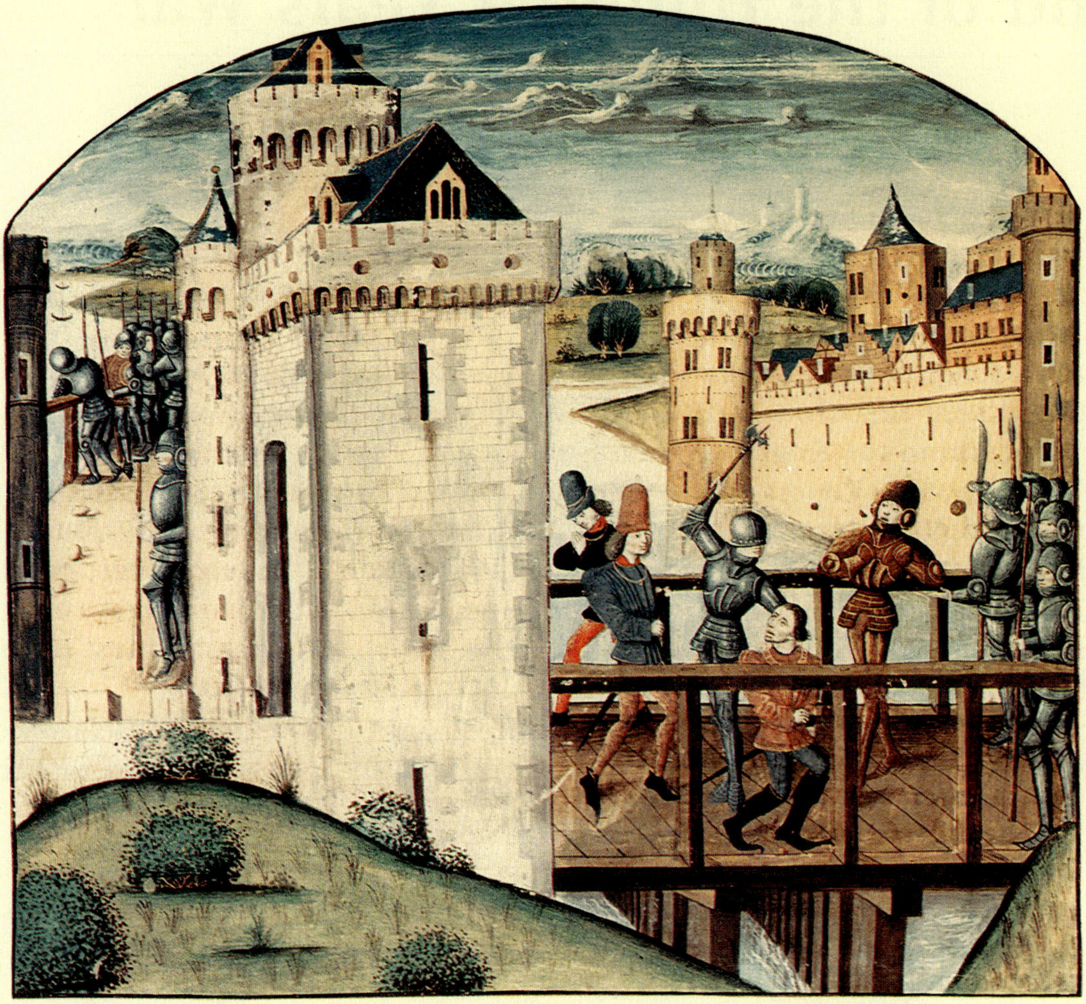

Figure 2 Murder of John the Fearless on the Bridge of Montereau

castle of Rougemont. Then, in October 1421, he attacked the town of Meaux. The siege lasted all through the winter, and many of the English died of disease. Meaux fell at last in March 1422, but Henry had caught an illness during the siege. He died soon afterwards. He never became King of France, as he had been promised by the Treaty of Troyes. Charles VI outlived him by six weeks.

When Henry V died, his son, Henry VI, was only a baby. But Henry V had chosen his brother, the Duke of Bedford to be Regent of France. Bedford was an able and determined man. He also had an excellent general, the Earl of Salisbury. Under these two men, the English armies had many successes. Their most important victory was in 1424 when they defeated the Dauphin's men at Verneuil. There were many Scots with the French army, and the English took great pleasure in killing them.

In 1428, Bedford and Salisbury laid siege to Orleans. This was a mistake. Orleans was strongly defended, and had a large garrison. As for the English, they did not have enough men to surround the town properly. It was not too difficult for the French to bring in reinforcements and supplies. Moreover, the English soon had a piece of bad luck. One day, a French school boy was wandering round the defences when he came upon a loaded cannon. Its crew had gone for lunch, and the boy could not resist firing the gun. The shot killed the Earl of Salisbury.

The siege of Orleans dragged on for months until, in April 1429, a French army came to relieve the town. With it was a remarkable young woman. Her name was Joan of Arc.

6 The End of the Hundred Years War

A Joan of Arc

Joan of Arc was born in about 1412, at the village of Domrémy in Lorraine. Her parents were ordinary peasants. Joan, however, was no ordinary girl. She decided that God had chosen her to save France from the English.

In 1419, Joan went to see Robert de Baudricourt. He was a nobleman who lived near her home. Joan persuaded de Baudricourt to give her an escort, and send her to the Dauphin, at Chinon. At first, the Dauphin and his advisers were very doubtful about Joan. How, they asked, could a peasant girl save France, when the greatest men in the country had failed? In the end, though, Joan convinced them that she could indeed drive out the English.

At that time, the English were besieging Orleans. The loss of the town would be a disaster for the French. Joan persuaded the Dauphin to send an army to relieve the place. Joan did not command the army, but she went with it. She did much to inspire the soldiers, and she led successful attacks on the English. Orleans was saved, and most people believed it was because of Joan.

After the French had relieved Orleans they pursued the English. Joan of Arc was with the

Figure 1 Joan of Arc. This is the only picture we have of Joan that was drawn when she was still alive.

Figure 2 (right) Joan of Arc before the Dauphin at Chinon

French. They caught and defeated the English at Patay. The English commanders were John, Lord Talbot and Sir John Fastolf. Talbot lost a third of his men and was himself captured. He had to pay a large ransom. He also had to promise that he would never again fight against the French in armour. He kept his promise, and always went into battle unprotected. You will see how he met his end on page 75.

After Patay, Joan told the Dauphin he must go to Rheims and be crowned King. Unwillingly, the Dauphin agreed. It was not just a question of travelling to Rheims. The country was in enemy hands, and the French had to storm several fortresses on their way. But they reached Rheims in safety, and the Dauphin was crowned King Charles VII. Joan stood by the King during the ceremony.

It is hard for us to understand how a young girl from a humble family could do so much. But Joan herself was quite sure of the reason. She said:

Document One

When I was thirteen years of age, I heard a voice from God to help me to know what to do. The first time, I was very frightened. This voice came about the middle of the day, in the summer, in my father's garden. I heard the voice upon my right side, from the direction of the church, and with it there was a bright light. After I had heard this voice three separate times, I realised it was the voice of an angel.

Everything I have done that was good, I did by command of my voices.

Procès de condamnation

1 How old was Joan when she first heard the voice?
2 How did she feel when she first heard it?
3 Whose voice did she decide it was?

At different times, Joan heard different voices. She claimed that usually it was St. Michael, St. Catherine or St. Margaret who was speaking to her. She said:

Figure 3 Joan of Arc directing a siege

Document Two

They taught me to lead a good life, and to go to church. They told me that I must go into France, and that I could no longer stay where I was. They told me that I would raise the siege of Orleans. They told me that I must go to the fortress city of Vaucouleurs, to find the captain of that place, Robert de Baudricourt. He would give me soldiers to go with me. I said I was a poor girl, who did not know how to ride a horse, or how to make war.

Procès de condamnation

1 What did Joan's voices teach her?
2 Where did they say she must go?
3 What victory did they say she would win? Who would help her?
4 How did Joan answer her voices?

As you have seen, Joan did all the things that her voices told her.

Before she went to war, the Dauphin gave Joan a suit of armour. But she refused the sword that he offered her. Instead, she sent for one that was hidden in the village church of Sainte-Cathérine-de-Fierbois. When she was asked how she knew it was there, she said:

Document Three

My voices told me. I wrote to the priests at that place to ask for the sword, and they sent it to me. It was not deep in the earth. It was, I think,

behind the altar. When the sword was found, it was rusty. But the priests rubbed it, and the rust came off easily. I was very fond of this sword, because it was found in the church of St. Catherine, whom I love so well.
Procès de condamnation

1 How did Joan know where the sword was? Where was it hidden?
2 Who cleaned it and sent it to Joan?
3 Why was Joan very fond of the sword?

Figure 4 Attacking a town with scaling ladders. This was how Joan's men took Saint-Pierre-le-Moûtier, after they had filled the ditch with faggots.

As one of the leaders of the army, Joan needed a standard. She said:

Document Four
My voices told me to take up the standard of God. Therefore I had my standard made with the image of Our Saviour on it. He was sitting in judgement among the clouds of the sky. With him was an angel holding a fleur-de-lys in his hand.
Procès de réhabilitation

1 What standard did Joan's voices say she should have?
2 Name some of the things that were on the standard. Draw a picture of the standard.

Someone who knew Joan well was a teacher at the University of Poitiers. He said:

Document Five
She prophesied to me, and to others who were with me, four things. First, she said that the English would be defeated, and that the siege that they had laid to Orleans would be raised. Then she said that the King would be crowned at Rheims. Thirdly, she said that the city of Paris would be returned to the King. Lastly, she said that the Duke of Orleans would come back from England. I have seen all these things come true.
Procès de réhabilitation

Note: The Duke of Orleans had been taken prisoner at the Battle of Agincourt.

1 How many events did Joan prophesy?
2 Did they come true?
3 What would you think of anyone who could foretell the future as well as Joan did?

A man who saw Joan riding off to war said:

Document Six
I saw her mount her horse, all in plain armour, but with no helmet. She had a little battle-axe in her hand. She had a big black charger. When she tried to mount it at the door of her inn, it reared up wildly, and would not let her. Then she said, 'Take him to the cross.' This was in front of a church, not far away. There she mounted. The horse never moved, but stood as if he was tied. She turned towards the church and said, 'You, the priests, make processions and prayers to God.' Then she turned once more upon her way, saying: 'Forward, forward!' Her standard was furled and carried by a gracious page, and she had her little battle-axe in her hand.
Chronique de la Pucelle

1 What was Joan wearing?
2 What was she carrying?
3 What happened when she first tried to mount her horse?
4 Where did she have the horse taken?
5 How did he behave there?
6 What did she tell the priests to do?

One of Joan's servants, Jean d'Aulon, described an attack on the town Saint-Pierre-le-Moûtier, in which Joan took part:

Document Seven
The town was very strong and it had many soldiers in it. They fought so well that the French had to retire. At that moment I arrived. I saw that the Maid had been left with very few men, and I was sure she would be killed or captured. I mounted a horse, and rushed towards her. I asked her what she was doing, all alone like that, and told her to retire like the rest. She said she was not alone, but still had 50,000 men with her. She refused to leave until she had taken the town.

In spite of what she said, she had no more than four or five men with her. I know for certain, and so do several others who also saw her. Therefore I told her to retire like the rest. But she told me to send for faggots to make a bridge over the moat. She shouted, 'Faggots, everybody, so that we can make a bridge!' And they were brought, and put in the moat. I was quite amazed, because the town was at once taken by assault, for this time the garrison hardly fought at all.
Procès de réhabilitation

Note: Joan of Arc was known as the Maid of Orleans.

1 Why had the French army retired?
2 What did d'Aulon tell Joan to do?
3 How many men did Joan say she had with her?
4 According to d'Aulon, how many did she have?
5 What did Joan ask for? Why?
6 What did Joan succeed in doing?

It is not surprising that some people began to think that Joan could work miracles. Here, though, is a description of her by Margaret de la Trémouille, a woman who knew her quite well:

Document Eight
She was in my house for three weeks, sleeping, eating and drinking. In all that time I never saw anything wrong. She behaved as an honest Christian woman. She went often to confession, heard Mass regularly, and frequently asked me to go to Matins. I went with her several times.

Sometimes we talked together. Once, someone said to Joan that, no doubt, she was not afraid to go into battle, because she was certain she would not be killed. She said she was no safer than anyone else.

I remember that several times women came to the house and brought rosaries, and other religious objects. They wanted Joan to touch them. This made her laugh, and she would say to me, 'Touch them yourself. They will be as good from your touch as they will from mine.'

Joan was generous in giving alms. She gave most willingly to the needy and poor, saying she had been sent to help them.

I am sure she was all innocence, expect in war. I saw her riding on horseback as the best of soldiers would have done. At that, the men-at-arms marvelled.
Procès de réhabilitation

Note: 'Mass' and 'Matins' – services of the Roman Catholic Church

1 What showed that Joan was a good Christian?
2 According to a visitor, why was Joan not afraid when she went into battle?
3 What did Joan reply?
4 What did women bring to the house? Why?
5 What did Joan say about this to Margaret de la Trémouille?
6 How did Joan treat the poor?
7 How did she surprise soldiers?

As you have already seen, Joan of Arc saved the city of Orleans, and saw the Dauphin

Figure 6 Joan chases a prostitute from the French camp

crowned at Rheims. After that, though, things began to go wrong. The French decided to try and capture Paris, believing the citizens would rise in their support. But the English defended the city well, and the citizens did not rise.

During the siege, Joan was unlucky enough to break her sword. This was not even fighting the English. She was chasing a prostitute out of the French camp when it happened. The King was very upset. He said to Joan, 'You should have taken a strong stick to the woman. Then, you would not have lost the sword which you say you had from God.'

The French made several attacks on Paris, but they failed. Joan herself was wounded in one of them. Soon, the French decided to raise the siege. The failure at Paris meant that the French King began to lose faith in Joan.

The following year, Joan heard that the Burgundians were besieging the town of Compiègne. She went at once to save the place. With her usual courage she led a sortie that took her right into the enemy camp. The

Burgundians were surprised, but they drove off their attackers. Moreover, in the fighting, one of them pulled Joan from her horse, and captured her. This was on May 23, 1340, only fifteen months since she had first met the Dauphin at Chinon.

The Burgundians sold Joan to the English. They were delighted to have such a dangerous enemy in their hands. Any other important French leader would have been freed, on payment of a ransom. But Joan was different. The English took her to Rouen, and put her on trial. They convicted her of witchcraft and heresy and burnt her alive. She was just nineteen years old. Charles VII, who owed his crown to her, had done nothing to try to save her.

In 1456 the French held a trial of another kind, which gave Joan back her good name. But it was not until 1920 that the Roman Catholic Church made her a saint.

Figure 7 The trial of Joan of Arc

Figure 8 Joan is burnt at the stake

B The Defeat of the English

Joan of Arc had hoped to drive the English from France. But when she died they still held almost all the land they had taken. Joan had had the Dauphin crowned at Rheims. Now it was the turn of the English. In 1431 the Regent, John, Duke of Bedford, took the nine year old Henry VI of England, to Paris. Here he was crowned Henry II of France. This child was the only person ever to be crowned King of both countries.

Figure 1
Philip the Good, Duke of Burgundy

During the next few years, the English more than held their own. But in 1435 there was a disaster for them. Philip the Good, Duke of Burgundy, gave up his alliance with England, and made an agreement with Charles VII of France. The English had conquered much of France, because her people had been fighting each other. One side, the Burgundians, had even helped the English. Now France was united, and the English had to fight alone.

In fact, the English held on surprisingly well. They lost Paris in 1436, but it was not until 1449 that the French were able to carry the war into Normandy. When they did, most of the towns fell, including the capital, Rouen. In a desperate attempt to save the province, the English government sent Sir Thomas Kyriell to France. This was in 1450. Kyriell landed his army at Cherbourg. He then marched to relieve Bayeux, which the French were besieging. On the way, he met a French army at Formigny and there was a battle. In Document One a Frenchman describes what happened:

Document One

The Count of Clermond and his men rode so hard that they caught up with the English near a village called Formigny. When the English saw them, they put themselves in line of battle. The two sides skirmished with each other for three hours. The English made large holes with their daggers and swords, so that the French and their horses should stumble if they charged them.

In the mean time, the Lord of Richemont, Constable of France, arrived with an army. The English saw them come, and they changed their position, for they were afraid of the Constable. Then Lord Clermond's troops charged the English, and so did those of the Constable. They attacked the English on both sides very bravely, so that in the end they defeated them.

According to the heralds, and the priests who buried them, there were killed three thousand seven hundred and seventy-four English. They were buried in fourteen trenches.

This day, only five or six of the French were slain. Our men fought very well, for there were only three thousand of them, while the English had from five to six thousand. Therefore wise men say that God gave the victory to the French.

Jacques le Bouvier, *Le Recouvrement de Normandie*

Notes: 'skirmish' – to fight, but not seriously
The Constable of France was the man in charge of all her armies

1 Look at the battle plan (Figure 3). Find:
   a. The Count of Clermond's troops.
   b. The first position of the English, when they fought with Clermond.
   c. The Constable's troops.
   d. The second position of the English, when they turned to face the Constable.
2 What did the English do to try to stop the French cavalry?
3 At what other battle had they done this? (If you have forgotten, read Document One, page 14.)

Figure 2 The Madonna and Chancellor Rolin, by Jan van Eyck. Rolin was Philip the Good's Chancellor. It was due, largely, to him, that France and Burgundy came to an agreement in 1435. Rolin is shown giving thanks to the Virgin for his success. King Charles VII admitted that he was responsible for the death of Philip's father, John the Fearless, on the bridge at Montereau. His excuse was that he had only been sixteen at the time. He agreed to put a cross on the bridge. You can see this in the background. He also promised to build a monastery, where monks would pray for John's soul. It is to the left of the bridge. Charles did not keep this part of his promise.

Figure 3 The Battle of Formigny

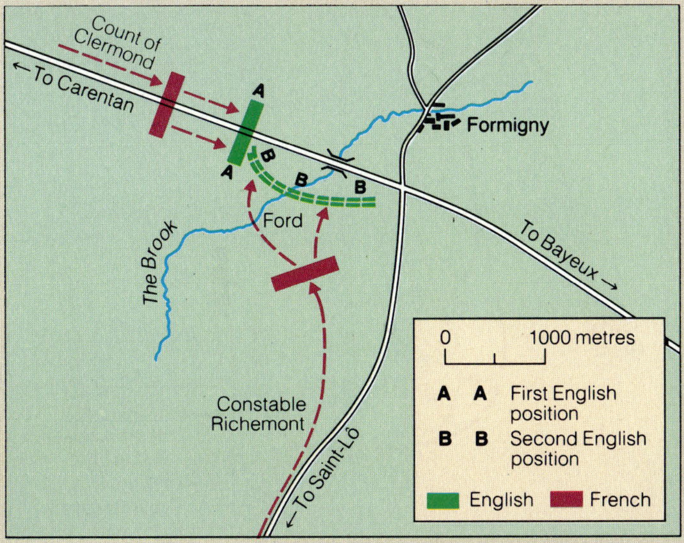

4 According to le Bouvier:

a. How many English were killed?

b. How many French were killed?

c. How many times, roughly, did the English outnumber the French?

d. What part did God play in the battle?

5 This document was, as you know, written by a Frenchman. Now read Document Ten, page 61. Compare what the Frenchman said about Formigny with what the Englishman said about Agincourt.

After Formigny, the French quickly took the whole of Normandy. The English were furious. They wanted a scapegoat, that is, someone to blame. They found him in one of their nobles, the Duke of Suffolk. He was accused of selling Normandy to the French, and many other crimes as well. A fortune-teller called Stacey told him that if he could escape from the dangers of the Tower, he would be safe. He was very relieved, therefore, when the the King had him taken from the Tower of London and banished to Calais.

But this is what happened on the way:

Document Two

He was sent on board a ship called the Nicholas of the Tower. And when he came, the captain greeted him with 'Welcome traitor!' He asked the sailors if they wished to help the Duke, but they said they would not in any way. He remembered what Stacey had told him, and his heart sank. Then he was taken out of the big ship into a boat. In it there was an axe and a block. One of the common sailors told him to lay down his head. He promised him he would be fairly treated, and die by the sword. And the man took a rusty sword, and hacked off his head with half a dozen strokes.

The Paston Letters

After the French had taken Normandy they went on and overran Gascony. Its capital, Bordeaux, fell in 1451. But the people of Bordeaux lived mainly from their wine trade with England. Also, they had been ruled by the Kings of England for three hundred years. They did not like being governed by the French. They told the English they would rebel, if they would send an army to help them. The English were pleased to send an army. Its leader was John, Lord Talbot. Talbot was over 70, but he was still very active. Also he was a famous soldier, and many of the French were scared of him.

Talbot arrived in Gascony in 1452. The people of Bordeaux rebelled as they had promised, and the French were driven from much of Gascony. They had been taken by surprise, but they came back with a large army the following year. They laid siege to the town of Castillon, and Talbot went to relieve the place. This is what happened:

Document Three

When the French knew Talbot was coming, they retreated to their camp, and prepared to defend themselves. The gunners mounted their cannons and culverins on the ditches facing the English.

The people of Castillon had told Talbot that if he advanced quickly, the French would flee. But when he arrived, he was surprised to see that it was not so. Instead, the French had fine fortifications with artillery, and were determined to fight.

Figure 4 Effigy of John Talbot

Figure 5 The Battle of Castillon

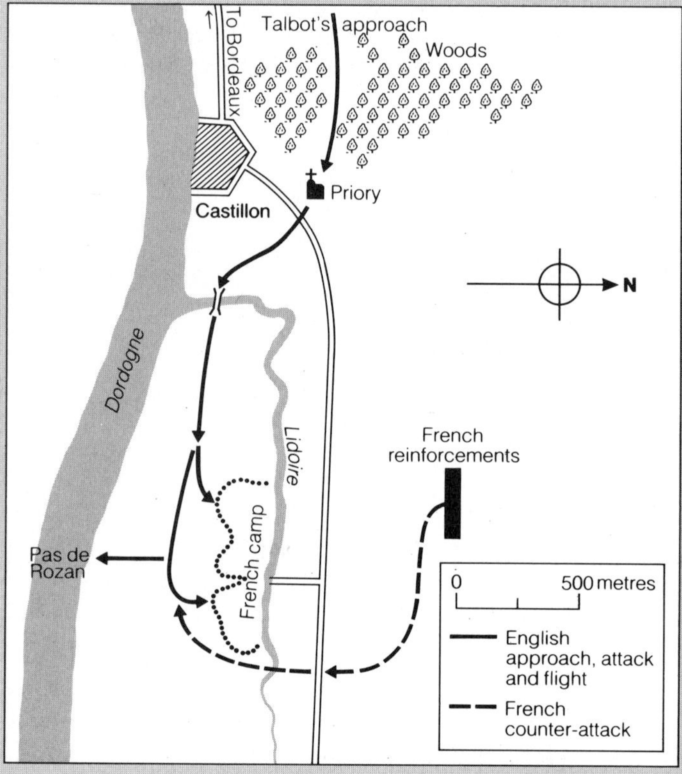

Figure 6 Artillery destroying the defences of a town

In this battle, Talbot was mounted on a little horse, because he was a very old man. But he made all his men fight on foot.

Then began a terrible attack, with both sides showing great bravery. There was hand to hand fighting, and marvellous struggles with axes and lances. This struggle lasted for an hour.

At last some French reinforcements arrived. They fought so well, with the aid of God, that the English turned their backs and fled. All their banners were thrown down, and they left many dead on the field. Talbot's horse was hit by a shot from a culverin, and dropped down dead. Talbot was thrown under it and was at once killed by some archers. So died this famous English leader. He had long been one of the most dangerous enemies of the French, and the dread and terror of France.

J. Chartier, *Chronique de Charles VII*

Note: 'culverin' – type of cannon. Or it could be a firearm about the size of a rifle, and held by a soldier

1 Where did the French go, when they heard Talbot was coming?

2 With what weapons did they prepare to defend themselves?

3 For how long did the English attack the French?

4 What happened soon after the French had reinforcements?

5 What happened to Talbot?

6 In this document you read about a kind of weapon that has not been mentioned much until now. What is it?

After the Battle of Castillon, it did not take the French long to overrun the whole of Gascony. Bordeaux surrendered, and its people had to make their peace with the King of France. There was no peace treaty with England, but, although no-one knew it, the Hundred Years War was over.

C Why the English were Defeated

During the Hundred Years War the English invaded France again and again. They captured many of her cities. They made chevauchées the length and breadth of the country. They won the few great battles that were fought. Yet in the end it was the French who won the war. In this section we must find out why.

You already know at least two reasons. One was the example set by Joan of Arc. It is true that she was not nearly as successful as she had hoped to be. None the less, she gave the French the will to fight, when they needed it most. The other reason was that in 1435 the English lost their Burgundian allies. The English could only hold much of France for as long as her people were fighting each other. Henry V owed far more to his Burgundian friends than he did to his victory at Agincourt. When the French stopped quarrelling among themselves, the English were bound, sooner or later, to be defeated.

There were other reasons as well. A French writer tells us one of them:

Document One

The King of France organised his men-at-arms

Figure 1 Charles VII of France in a procession

so well that it was a fine thing to see. He gave all these men-at-arms good armour and weapons. They all had armour for their bodies and their limbs, helmets and swords.

They also had lances, carried by their pages. Each one had three good horses, one for himself, one for his page, and one for his servant. The pages and servants were armed with helmets, hauberks, daggers and axes. Each of the men-at-arms had with him two mounted archers. They were armed with hauberks and helmets.

These men-at-arms were paid each month. They did not dare to take any of the ordinary French people prisoner, nor to take any of their animals or food without paying for them.
J. Chartier, *Chronique de Charles VII*

Note: 'hauberk' – jacket of chain mail. The men-at-arms had plate armour.

1 What armour and weapons did the French King give his men-at-arms?
2 How many men did each man-at-arms have with him? Make a list of them, and give the armour and weapons of each.
3 How did all these men travel?
4 What happened every month?
5 How did the French soldiers behave, as a result?

Figure 2 Charles VII of France and his court

For much of the Hundred Years War, the kings of France had had to rely for their armies on the feudal levy. This was the nobles, who were unpaid, and the men they brought to war at their own expense. A huge force could be raised in that way, but it was nearly impossible to discipline it. The men were not paid by the king, so they did much as they pleased. It was armies like this which lost the battles of Crécy, Poitiers and Agincourt.

But, as you have seen in Document One, towards the end of the Hundred Years War, the French army was different. It was made up of professional soldiers, paid by the King. The king had the men under his control, so he could discipline them. For example, there were no more wild charges led by nobles who were anxious to show off. Also, since the men were paid, they had no need to plunder the countryside for food. Hitherto, the French armies had treated the ordinary folk almost as badly as the English did. Now, the French armies paid for what they took, while the English went on robbing, burning and murdering. If you were a French peasant, how would you feel about the English soldiers? How would you feel about the French? What are some of the things you might do, if you heard an English army was coming? What might you do, if you knew that it was a French one?

There was yet another reason why the French won the Hundred Years War:

Document Two

The French King had an enormous amount of artillery. He owned very many great bombards, great cannons, veuglaires, serpentines, crapaudins, culverins, and ribaudquins. No king ever had so many guns, so many carriages to drag them, so much powder and shot, and so many gunners. The men who organised this artillery were Master John Bureau, Treasurer of France, and his brother, Jaspar Bureau, general of the artillery.

It was a marvellous thing to see the mounds, ditches and mines that the Bureau brothers made before the towns and castles that they besieged. Because of their skill, they could have taken any place they wanted, by force of arms. But when any of these places was about to fall, the King always wanted to accept its surrender. He did so out of kindness, to avoid the shedding of human blood and the destruction of his own country.

J. Chartier, *Chronique de Charles VII*

1. How many different kinds of gun are mentioned here?
2. What did the King have with them?
3. Who organised the artillery?
4. What siege works did they make when attacking a place?
5. What would the King rather do, than take a place by storm? Why?

Figure 3 Attacking a camp with artillery

Figure 4 Portrait of Charles VII

Figure 5 Statue of Jean Bureau

Guns were not new. As you have seen, Henry V used them at the siege of Harfleur. But in about 1430, there was an important invention. This was the powder mill. Gunpowder is made from sulphur, saltpetre and carbon. At first, these ingredients were mixed on the battle field. It was a bit like taking the flour, sugar and eggs on your picnic and making your cakes when you arrived. The powder mill mixed the ingredients and formed the gunpowder into little pellets, about the size of grains of wheat. During a battle, this could be poured straight into the guns. It was like going on a picnic, with your cakes already made.

Moreover, Charles VII of France had the services of John Bureau. Bureau was from an ordinary family, but he became an expert on artillery. He discovered how to make better guns than anyone else, and how to use them in battles and sieges. Charles VII had the good sense to see how important Bureau's work was. He gave Bureau all the money he needed, and Bureau gave the King the finest artillery in Europe.

The French had two guns at Formigny which fired on the English archers from a safe distance. In the end, the archers had to break their ranks to capture the guns. The French had far more firearms at Castillon. This was a battle between guns and archers, and the guns won.

But Bureau's guns were more important for sieges. They would batter down the strongest walls quite easily. Defenders knew this, and when they found themselves besieged by Bureau, they were quick to surrender. The English had taken the towns and castles of Normandy one by one, over many years. Bureau recaptured them all in a few months.

We can think of the French fortunes during the later years of the Hundred Years War as the movement of the tide. In the time of Henry V the sea went out a long way. Charles VI even agreed that on his death, Henry, rather than his own son, should become King of France. Then, because of Joan of Arc, the tide turned. The sea went out no further, but, for the moment, it did not come in to cover the sands. That happened in the reign of Charles VII, the man Charles VI had disinherited! It was thanks, largely, to his master gunner, Jean Bureau.

Figure 1 Calais

D Epilogue

After the Battle of Castillon and the loss of Gascony, the English gave up the struggle. They had made enormous efforts, which had cost them many lives. They had devastated vast areas of France, and had butchered many thousands of French people, especially unarmed peasants. They had had their great triumphs, such as Crécy, Poitiers and Agincourt. At one time, much of France was under their rule. When the war ended, however, all that was left of the great English empire was the town of Calais. In 1558, even Calais was lost. But the Kings of England went on calling themselves Kings of France until 1802.